THE GOD WHO HEALS

Yesterday, Today, and Tomorrow

Dr. Georgianne Summer

FOREWORDS BY DR. DERRICK SNODGRASS & LA TOIJA SNODGRASS

WORD & SPIRIT
PUBLISHING

Please note the author's style which capitalizes certain pronouns that refer to the Father, Son, and Holy Spirit, and may differ from other publishers' styles. Take note that the name satan and related names are not capitalized, as we choose not to acknowledge him, even to the point of violating rules of grammar.

Cover Photo Courtesy of Cari Gillespie Tietsort Photography

The God Who Heals: Yesterday, Today, and Tomorrow

ISBN: 98-1-685730-30-7

Published by Word and Spirit Publishing
P.O. Box 701403
Tulsa, Oklahoma 74170
wordandspiritpublishing.com

Printed in the United States of America.

Contents

Foreword

Dr. Derrick Snodgrass Jr.

IN GEORGIANNE'S BOOK, *The God Who Heals: Yesterday, Today, and Tomorrow*, she takes you on an amazing journey of healing and restoration for your own personal life. I've had the privilege of knowing Georgianne, and one of the things that became apparent at first contact was her burden to see the Body of Christ healed and walking in wholeness. Georgianne first reached out to me as I was teaching a series on healing at my church. Every week, I could feel the overflow of joy and hopefulness in her as the words being spoken each week strongly resonated with her convictions. Georgianne does a masterful job at articulating the sentiments of her heart in a way that is practical and easily understood. Scripture says in Revelation 12:11, "They overcame him by the blood of the Lamb and by the word of their testimony" (NKJV). The Greek word for *testimony is marturia*, which means "evidence." The blood of Jesus married to our testimony gives us the ability to overcome satan. It is the evidence of God in your life that will cause people to overcome! Georgianne does a wonderful job of taking Scripture passages and merging them with her own personal testimony. She's been through so much, and she has a wealth of knowledge and inspiration that will leave you speechless at times and on the very edge of your seat! Georgianne dares to tackle the difficult things, the hard things, and she crushes stigmas and errant belief systems that have infiltrated the church. In this trampling of the hard things, we get the essence, and the joy, much like grapes when they are pressed produce wine! I'm persuaded that upon reading this book, some things will challenge you, ignite you, but most of all encourage you. Her prayer is that you are healed in mind, body, and Spirit, and that you don't accommodate sickness in any form. What I loved about reading this book is that most of the questions that cause us to doubt the healing power of God are our personal experiences. Georgianne will guide you with Scriptures and by her journey, combating most of the big topics that trigger doubt in the believer's heart. This is a book you will not want to stop reading, and you will want to share it with others. Be encouraged by the revelation in *The God Who Heals: Yesterday, Today, and Tomorrow*!

Dr. Derrick Snodgrass Jr.
Lead Pastor of Willow Church

Foreword

La Toija Snodgrass

THE GOD WHO Heals: Yesterday, Today, and Tomorrow is a sincere dive into the heart of Georgianne, who has experienced personal sickness, sickness of loved ones, premature death of loved ones, and unimaginable loss. Yet she transparently walks the reader through her journey of seeking, as she highlights truth about the Father God's will to heal His children! Tackling misconceptions about God's desire to heal, from the Old Testament all the way to the present day, Georgianne dares to address our questions and answer them with the Word of God. She employs Scripture to thoroughly explain how healing brings God glory! This book will provide pragmatic steps to seeing healing in your everyday life and ministry. You will learn how to denounce the enemy's devices against receiving healing. God wants us to be whole in our mind, body, and soul.

Interestingly, Georgianne is a Doctor of Nursing and a nurse practitioner, and she understands the role of medicine in prolonging the life of humankind, yet she is determined not to allow this knowledge to challenge her faith as a believer. Although not directly in the medical field, I share Georgianne's sentiment regarding seeing disease as well as physical, emotional, and mental sickness through man's eyes. As an epidemiologist, I am called upon to share the facts about disease, its spread, and the varying propensities on diverse populations. However, I recognize that the *fact* is not synonymous with the *truth*. It is apparent that Georgianne and I share this stance. She is first and foremost a child of God and has done a marvelous job of explaining and teaching healing through the lens of God! I'm honored to be a small part of the big work God will do through these writings.

La Toija Snodgrass
Author, Leader, and Prophetess

Introduction

WHAT IF YOU had at your disposal the greatest physician that ever was? What if he had a 100 percent track record for healing all disease, sickness, and pain? Would you use that physician, or would you go to an average physician who knows only in part, who is good at what he does but only has a track record of 50 percent or maybe even 80 percent? Would you take your chances with the latter, or would you choose the former?

Well, we have available to us the Great Physician, the Creator of our bodies, the one who knows the problem and how to correct it! However, we often fail to ask Him for help until we have tried every other source. There is nothing wrong with seeking medical attention; I am not against medications, doctors, or some alternative modalities. I have been a medical professional for almost twenty years now, and it was God who called me to that role. Because of that role, sometimes my medical mind goes unchecked, and it gets me into trouble when I allow it to override my spiritual mind. One day, while I was taking over-the-counter medicine for a headache, God said to me, "You're not even going to ask Me about this pain?" At that moment, I realized that too often, we don't even ask the One who created us about our pain; we just grab what we know will work. That last statement is a problem, because it indicates we do not believe that God works.

We can say whatever we want, but our actions are the evidence of what we truly believe. Could it be we just haven't tested Him or tried Him in this area? He tells us to call the elders to anoint and pray for the sick (see James 5:14–16); could it be we just aren't following the directions in the Bible? God tells us, "Be anxious for nothing, but in everything by prayer and supplication with thanksgiving let your requests be made known to God. And the peace of God, which surpasses all comprehension, will guard your hearts and your minds in Christ Jesus" (Philippians 4:6–7). So many people are running around holding on to their anxiety, that panic attacks have become commonplace.

God is clearly still in the healing business, which is why missionaries still tell stories of those who have been healed, delivered, and who witnessed the supernatural power of God. In third-world countries, where there is little or no access to healthcare, they pray first, and they expect God to answer, because He is their only source. They follow what the Bible says, because it is their only prescription.

Here in America, most people have access to medications, healthcare providers, emergency rooms, clinics, specialists, and so on. (I am aware that our healthcare system is badly broken, which is why I say "most.") When we have a headache, we grab Tylenol, ibuprofen, or a prescription we have been given, and we expect the headache to go away. We continue treating ourselves, or we seek a healthcare provider to treat us, until the treatment doesn't work or there is no cure. Only at that point, when all else fails us, do we turn to God and ask for His help. But that is backward! We should seek Him first, and then do what it is He tells us to do about the problem.

Now I know you are thinking that God gave us physicians and the knowledge to create medicine, so He expects us to use what He gave us. Yes, He did, and He heals through these avenues, and we are grateful. However, we do not have to choose between these two courses of action (unless God Himself instructs you to do so). I know that without His provision of medicine and of those who practice it, I would have been dead long before I found God and His truths about healing. Remember that God's main goal is always our salvation (which, by the way, includes healing), so He wants us to stay alive physically until He can reach us spiritually. He knew that many would leave their earthly bodies before He could get His truth to them. In His mercy, He gave humankind the knowledge needed to treat and prevent illness. We can actually see God doing this as far back as the Old Testament, with the Law of Moses. More recently, He gave humankind the ability to keep the body alive in the face of disease and sickness. However, this area is also where Western medicine fails many times. Our healthcare system was created to treat the symptoms of illness but not correct the root of the issue. Those who work within that system are doing the best they can. Now we have millions of people who are still sick walking around thinking they are healthy and taking medicine never meant to cure anything. Many times, these people experience worse side effects from treatments than they did from the original illness.

God is the Creator, and He knows the body far better than we do. He even created it to heal itself! Therefore, He should be the first person we turn to, not our last hope. Whether we take medication, seek medical professionals, or battle it out in prayer, the main thing is to seek Him first. We must ask our Creator what we should do concerning our body, any sickness, or disease, and He will direct our path. Whichever direction He leads us is the direction we should go, and then we must go in faith.

Think how silly it would be to take medication without an expectation that it would work. Why would I even consider taking something I had no faith in? At the same time, if I have no faith that God heals, or if I believe that He gave me the sickness, or if I doubt that He wants to heal me, why would I ask Him? No matter what we believe, our beliefs and actions must line up in order to work. This applies to *all* beliefs—and this was a new revelation to me after forty-two years of Christianity. We can say what we believe (or think we believe) all we want, but what we truly believe is what we act upon. One of my favorite Generals, Smith Wigglesworth, said it this way: "I am not moved by what I see. I am moved only by what I believe."[1] I encourage you to read Romans 14 (some Bibles outline it as the "Principles of Conscience"), as it gives insight into our choices lining up with our faith.

We must also remember not to judge others for the route they choose in their personal healing. Each person must act according to their own faith, because trying to live by someone else's faith does not work. God meets people in different places, and not all walks will be the same; there is no judgment or condemnation allowed here. I am merely sharing truths from the God I know and love. This book was written to help us to understand healing, to be healed, and to stay healed.

I hope you keep reading, as we are going to talk about God's will to heal and Jesus' ministry of healing. We'll also debunk some wrong teachings concerning healing, share stories of personal healings, and give you a list of Scripture passages about healing.

[1] Smith Wigglesworth, quoted in Roberts Liardon, ed., *God's Generals: Why They Succeeded and Why Some Failed* (Tulsa, OK: Albury Publishing, 1996), 211. Used by Permission.

CHAPTER 1

Who Am I?

LET ME SHARE with you the short version of my life and how I got here, writing a book on healing. First and foremost, I am a daughter of the Most High God, and like everyone, I have many roles in my earthly life. I am a child, a wife, a mother, a nurse, a nurse practitioner, a Doctor of Nursing (which tends to be the biggest opponent to my faith), and a university professor. Similar to many of you reading this book, I am really just a being walking this earth for a visit, trying to learn how to exemplify my God in all that I do and speak.

I do not tell you those things to brag about myself; actually, it's the opposite. I would not have accomplished anything in this life had it not been for God. In all the roles I have played, I sometimes lost track of Him and of myself as His daughter. I can look back now and easily see how the Lord has worked in my life from the earliest age. I see how He has been faithful to me even when I was not faithful to Him.

I was three years old when I discovered the fighter in me and became a defender of those who could not speak for themselves. Even in elementary school, I had both a passion and compassion inside of me for the frail, the hurting, and the sick. This passion has never left me, and it still motivates me. All of us have, on some level, witnessed death, pain, sickness, and crippling fear. I have prayed with families and cried with them. I have held the hands and bodies of those leaving this earth. I have also witnessed and been a part of miracles, healings, and touches of God, yet I am not a minister by trade, nor do I daily walk in the atmosphere of the miraculous (though that is my heart's desire).

Inside me there has always been a sense of wonder and amazement about God and a desire to see Him show up and do things like He did in the Bible. I had an awareness of God from an early age, and I was raised in church by a mother who knew God well. As a matter of fact, most of my family loved God, knew Him, and followed Him to the best of their abilities. Although each person's perspective on God was a little different, their foundations were all the same. I love my roots, but no one, at least no one I knew aside from my mother, and later her brothers, really believed miracles still happened or should be expected. At the age of nine, on the floor of a tiny church off a dirt road, I asked Him into my heart. I thought, possibly like many of you, that life was going to be perfect from this point forward: my dad would be saved and start coming to church, my family would be healed, and I would excel in school with lots of friends. However, things did not begin to go perfectly after this time; as a matter of fact, the devil unleashed all sorts of evil things in my life in the form of abuse, predators, isolation, and school bullies. During some of the scariest times of my childhood, I would sit in my room or my brother's room to pray and sing. I just knew there was supposed to be more in this life than all the pain, and I knew that God didn't intend for these things to happen. Let me clarify that I didn't tell a soul about what was happening to me, and my family had no idea until I shared with them years later. A child's mind can be a confusing place, and I could give reasons why I didn't, but I wanted you to know that they would have intervened had I said something.

I want to pause this story here for a moment and explain about my mom, her faith in God, and His intervention at my birth. In 1969, while pregnant with me, my mother, who was a spirit-filled Baptist and a spiritual warrior like no one I have ever known (I imagine the devil hated every day she woke up, because he had tried to kill her multiple times), worked in an area that was testing influenza variants. Multiple times a day, she walked through the testing lab to go to the bathroom. She had no issues with the viruses, no sickness, so signs or symptoms at all, and no reason to fear for me. On February 27, 1970, I came into the world so sick that the hospital staff did not even allow my mother to touch or see me. They told her I would die within a few hours. My death certificate was signed (not by my mom), and they placed me in isolation within the NICU on the third floor. The hospital staff were the only ones who could see me, and no one expected me to live. However, my mom was a praying woman, she had two older brothers who were pastors, and they all knew how to pray. Though she could not see me or hold me, she stood her ground and continued telling the medical staff that I was going to live and not die, because God had promised her a daughter and I was her. She called her brothers and her own church pastor and told them to get everyone to pray. I think there was at least half of Georgia and a part of Texas praying for me.

You see, I was born septic and would need a complete blood transfusion before I was safe. The doctors did not know what caused the sepsis, but God did, and He told my mom one night in the hospital. He reminded her of how she walked through the lab to go to the bathroom, and He told her to call the General (she was his secretary) and have him send the antidote to whatever they were working on. God answered all those prayers and fulfilled the promise He gave to my mom, and I lived. I had a few health issues that required medical care and multiple surgeries over the next six years, but they were minor in comparison. Then, at the age of fourteen, God healed those as well.

When I was fourteen years old, I asked my mother to take me to Savannah, Georgia, where Oral Roberts and his son Richard were holding a crusade. That was my first encounter with a Healing General of the Faith. I dreamed of going to ORU and healing the sick from that day forward. Since then, I have learned of other Healing Generals such as Smith Wigglesworth, the "Apostle of Faith"; Maria Woodworth Etter, an American Healing Evangelist; and John G. Lake, of whom it was scientifically documented that the black plague virus died the moment it came into contact with his skin.

These were not people of the Bible, but they came long after; they had faith, with actions, that saw real results. The more I studied, the more I wanted to discover what was different. What had we lost? Clearly, something was missing, because we just don't see the same results, even though we are declaring the same Scriptures. I know that neither the Scriptures nor God has changed. There are many other healers whom I have discovered in the last couple of years of study; we will talk about them later. For now, let's return to my childhood.

The life I dreamed of as a child, as a caped crusader, did not go as planned. Since those childhood years I have had moments, even seasons, in which I lost the fight inside. They were times of fear, doubt, anger, excuses, and self-pity, but God didn't leave me or allow me to remain there. He always found a way to reach me and bring me back into His loving arms. I just love how God loves us and guides us back, time and time again.

One of the greatest challenges to my faith came after I was married and became a mother at a very young age. Scientists discovered that the disease that had torn my husband's world apart as a teenager wasn't the disease we thought it was; it was worse. Not only was he in danger, but our three little boys were too. My husband, Mike, came to know the Lord in 1995, and life was actually wonderful. Again, I thought that life would be perfect now, since I thought that the Christian life was supposed to lead me to a war-free zone (did I mention I was young?). The Lord had been teaching Mike and me what marriage was about and how to love each other the way God intended, instead of battling through our broken pasts and erroneous expectations. However, in 1999, our lives would forever change when the disease hit Mike hard and he would lose his final job. I would need to be the income provider in our household. (I know now that God is the provider; jobs are merely sources.) In hindsight, I realize that the disease had actually already been evident for years, but we were in denial, and denial really can be a good place on occasion. But when a neurological disease is so obvious that the top specialist in that field takes one look at you in a hallway and confirms your thoughts, it's pretty bad. I can still see Mike that day in the hallway, and I remember that my faith was trying to rise up inside me, saying, "Well, at least now we know how to pray." In reality, however, now I had to battle facts, not just thoughts, and my faith level wasn't there yet!

Two weeks after Mike's official diagnosis of Huntington's Disease, I was headed on a mission trip to Zambia, Africa. God had ordained this trip earlier in the year, and it was too late to back out. I remember praying all the way there, because I didn't know what to do; my current job wouldn't support our family of five. I enjoyed school and I hated that I didn't graduate, but I had survived being a teen mom and had never considered a career since my boys were born. I had seven life-changing days with our team and with a missionary couple who were a doctor and nurse in outlying villages. I had an answer now, and I knew God wanted me to go to nursing school. I returned home from Africa a changed person, blessed beyond all I could imagine on that trip, and I enrolled in pre-nursing courses. When God has a plan and we are in tune with Him, all things are possible. I was accepted into Emory School of Nursing. After graduating and beginning my career as a nurse, I realized that while I wanted to care for people, I also wanted to lay hands on my patients and see them recover. I longed to see God show up in those hospitals and to empty out my assigned unit. I thought of how amazing it would be to be like Peter, walking along and having his shadow heal those in his path.

Unfortunately, with all that was about to happen, I would lose sight of God's promises in my everyday life. Eventually, I stopped praying for my patients, unless their families requested it. I allowed workplace culture, facts, science, sickness, and death to become more real to me than God's Word. Then, on August 23, 2007, my middle son was diagnosed with the same disease that we were going through with his father, except his version was much worse. I was already so tired of the fight; I was constantly working with disease and death at the hospital, and now I was surrounded at home too. I tried to keep faith, but I lost my focus on the Lord and the sight of His promises. God never meant for us to walk this earthly life alone, without those of like faith surrounding us. However, getting us alone is exactly what our enemy desires, and I played right into it. The worse life appeared, the more isolated I became. If he can isolate us, he can whisper those seeds of doubt into our ears. Once they are planted, it only takes a few events for them to grow like weeds.

One of those events was the day that a pastor, beloved friend, and mentor to Chris died prematurely of cancer. On the way home from the memorial service, Christopher turned to me and said, "Mom, if God didn't heal Pastor *Perry,* then why on earth would He heal me?" I did not have an answer; I only reminded him (and myself) of the promises of God's healing. However, inside I was full of doubt and mourning the loss of another great man of God who should not have died so young! I did not know it then, but I was riding on my mother's coattail of faith, and my foundation wasn't as solid as I thought. I wanted to believe, I tried to believe, but I had done this already, so I knew what to expect medically. My focus was more on the disease and its symptoms. Add to that the wrong beliefs and weariness from battle, and I was just trying not to drown.

Not long after that day, I lost hope. I had a husband dying in a nursing home more than two hours away, one son dying with a worse version of the same disease, one son off in the middle of a war, and another in high school contending with all of this alone.

I stopped attending church, because what I believed in so much wasn't manifesting as I knew it should. I was utterly disappointed in God and all those who called themselves Christians. Why was there no one healing the sick and raising the dead? Why wasn't I? There was no one around me who believed like I did, and my faith was failing me. I also couldn't take one more line of the stupid things people say when they don't know what to say. No, this was not my son's time to go, nor would God receive glory in this sickness. Christopher was not going to be an angel, and he was not needed more in heaven than on earth. I was hurting, and if one more person told me, "God is teaching you a lesson," I was going to punch them (which is a bad thing to do in church). I will address these wrong beliefs later.

At this point, deep depression had set in. I pretty much lived in my bedroom when I wasn't working. I still talked to God, though I am positive I was not listening to Him, nor was I very reverent (I do not recommend this approach, though God will handle it). I would talk to God, venting and telling Him how angry and hurt I was that I had lost my precious Mike to this horrid disease and that my middle son's body was failing him even faster than his dad's was. But nothing could prepare me for the day I watched my son leave this world for the next. Christopher and I lost this battle one month and one day after his twenty-eighth birthday, just three short years after his father's death. It would take some time before I would realize how blessed our family was in spite of this horrid disease, as I knew families who lost all their children to this genetic evil, some even in their young childhood years.

The war between what I knew about God and His promises, and the fact that I was not seeing those things manifest in my life or those around me, raged within me for almost three years. The God I loved and trusted was the one I was so angry at and so disappointed in. Where do you go when you are angry with the One person who is on your side? The One person who can help? The One who got you through everything up to this moment? You go to places you shouldn't or to people you shouldn't. You hide yourself in work, or you remain in a perpetual state of mourning. Even while I was not where I needed to be, God was right where I left Him, still reaching out and waiting for me. Although I couldn't see Him through all the pain, He was still working on my behalf. Then, in an instant, three years after Chris's death, God healed me of all the pain, anger, and disappointment. When we are going through trials and pain, it is sometimes difficult to see the goodness of God unless we are trained to do so, which I was not (yet). Although He was about to show me.

A close friend had told me about a revival happening in Dawsonville, Georgia. She told me about the miracles happening and the presence of God in the North Georgia Revival (NGR). At first, I was angry at this. Where was this when I needed it? I didn't go the first time she told me about it. I actually didn't go until the following year, after I realized that life without God was not an option. I needed to find again the God I loved and had known most of my life. If He was showing up there, then that was where I was going to start my search.

On February 24, 2019, my mom and I walked into the service at NGR, and I heard God speak again, so clearly. I knew that voice, and I was so relieved when I heard it, but I was still angry. My spirit began to rise inside me, and I knew that if I could just get in those waters, God would remove all of the anger, because He was the only one who could. We could not stay for baptism that night because Mom had to get home, so I would have to come back the following week. I felt some relief at having heard God again, and He assured me that we had an appointment.

I returned on March 3, 2019, with the only intention of getting into those waters, where I knew God would heal all the pain, grief, regret, and torment I was going through. As I sat praying, waiting for my turn in the baptismal waters, I had no idea what was about to happen. Then, the moment my foot first entered the water, all that grief came wailing out. I was sobbing so hard. I had never experienced anything like it; I could feel it coming out in waves. I got to the pastor, who asked, "What brings you into the water?" I could not speak; I was still sobbing so hard. He simply said, "Take your time; we will wait. We are not in a hurry here." After a few minutes went by, I told him about the disease and deaths, all the torment, pain, anger, and disappointment I had in God, how I didn't know how to let it go, and how God was the only one who could take it away. Pastor Marty prayed over me, and then quickly down into the water I went. When I came up, I felt clean, not angry, and free of the overwhelming grief. I remember a lady holding me gently as I floated there in the pool, stroking my hair and praying over me. It was a healing moment, a glorious moment; it was a God moment. Not only did God take all the emotional torment, but He also healed me of major depressive disorder (MDD). I had received that diagnosis shortly after graduating from nursing school, but I discovered that I had experienced it since childhood. That probably shouldn't have surprised me, given all that happened in my early years, my recent losses, and my failure to talk with anyone about it. God restored me instantly to Himself and completely healed my mind.

What I knew in my earlier years was based on the way I was raised. I had heard many religious peoples' beliefs about healing, and I didn't really know what to believe. Deep down, I had a feeling that God would still do "Bible things"; I just didn't know how. At the age of twenty-five, I realized that I needed to know what God said about healing, and not what my mom, my pastor, or I thought about it. I began searching, but I had very few Scriptures in my heart, so I couldn't battle the enemy for myself.

These are just a few examples of the manifestations of God's healing power in my life. They were all surrounded by different circumstances and occurred in different ways. God doesn't do it the same way every time. Jesus shows that through His ministry as well. What we must know beyond a shadow of doubt is that it is always

God's will to heal, just as it is His will that none should perish without salvation. Whether we see it manifested on this earth or not, the truth remains unchanged. I think about it like this: God's truth, like gravity, is working all the time. Whether we believe it or not, it does not change. Therefore, I know that the failure to see biblical truth manifested in my life is on my side, not on God's.

CHAPTER 2

God's Will to Heal: Old Testament Evidence

Learning to Study the Bible

THE GREAT HEALING evangelist F. F. Bosworth said, "Faith begins where the will of God is known."[2] How do we know God's will? Actually, this is an easier question to answer than many realize. He provided us with His will and testament written by men inspired by the Holy Spirit. An amazing teacher, Dr. Karen Smith, taught me that the Old Testament is God's story of unchanging love and pursuit of us, and the New Testament is the will and testament of Jesus signed and sealed in His blood. This changed the way I saw the Bible; it gave me a hunger to read all of it. Now as I read, I discover new things almost daily. The Bible truly is the living Word; therefore, when we read it, we will learn God's will, and we can (and should) ask Him to help us understand it.

Our knowledge and understanding of Scripture is essential to our walk on this earth, which is why we are instructed to "meditate on it day and night" (Joshua 1:8) and to "hide it in our hearts" (see

[2] F. F. Bosworth, quoted in Roberts Liardon, ed., *God's Generals: The Healing Evangelists* (New Kensington, PA: Whitaker House, 2011), 37. Used by Permission.

Psalm 119:11). Remember that Jesus defeated satan in the wilderness with the Word, and each time He was tempted, He quoted Scripture. Jesus said to satan, "It is written . . ." If Jesus the Living Word quoted the written Word to defeat the enemy, how much more are we going to need to know how to do this? However, I didn't know all of this until recently, so I no longer allow myself to sit pondering with thoughts of what could have been or what should have been, or with wishing I knew then what I know now.

After my experience in the waters, I was learning, reading, and writing Scriptures daily. I was building my faith and a Scripture base, which is like building an arsenal in preparation for battle. I am thankful God planted a strong sense in me to ask why, and I don't believe that is a bad question (although you must be ready for the answer). This inner detective has served me well in many areas but specifically in nursing, and now it served me well in studying the Bible.

One of the best lessons Dr. Smith taught me during my time at Kineo Ministry Training Center was how to use *Strong's Exhaustive Concordance* and how to cross-reference Scripture passages. She also taught me that the Scriptures point to one another, and they are not just a grouping of independent thoughts. This reframing cleared the filters through which I had read the Bible my whole life. Knowing these things gave me a better understanding and a way to study any topic. Healing was at the top of my list of topics, so I again began asking God, seeking His Word for answers, and this time I expected Him to show me.

My faith had been stripped bare and was being rebuilt from a place of a strong foundation. I asked according to Matthew 7:7, "Ask, and it will be given to you; seek, and you will find; knock, and it will be opened to you." I also expected to be taught according to 1 John 2:27, which tells us that the Holy Spirit within us teaches us all things as we abide in Him (paraphrased). Jesus also taught us to abide in Him in the parable He told in John 15 of the vine and branches. I love how all of Scripture is woven together like a tapestry.

Strong's lists 155 Scripture passages that mention *heal, healed, healer, healeth, healing(s),* and *health,* and the New Testament consists of 78 of that total number. So, if it wasn't God's will to heal the sick, why would He have put so many passages about the subject in the Bible? Most people refer to the New Testament when they speak of healing, but we can see God's will to heal throughout the Bible. I want to share six stories of healing from the Old Testament, and I will begin with the book of Genesis.

Old Testament Proof

My favorite biblical patriarch, Abraham, was more than a character in a song; he was a man chosen by God. He truly believed in God's faithfulness so much that he was willing to sacrifice his own child. That level of faith is why he is my favorite person in the Bible besides Jesus. Abraham was a considered a "Friend of God" (James 2:23 KJV). Through his faith in God, he became the father of the faith. He was the first person we see able to persuade God to change His plans (see Genesis 18); in this chapter, Abraham shows us how to intercede on the behalf of others. Later, in Genesis 20:17 (NLT), he prayed to God on behalf of King Abimelech: "Then Abraham prayed to God, and God healed Abimelech, his wife, and his female servants, so they could have children."

Moses was the second patriarch we read about who was able to persuade God by interceding with Him, and Moses even spoke with God face-to-face. Moses interceded for the children of Israel several times, but on one particular occasion, he was interceding on behalf of his sister after she and Aaron attempted to overthrow him. "Moses cried out to the LORD, saying, 'O God, heal her, I pray!' But the LORD said to Moses, 'If her father had but spit in her face, would she not bear her shame for seven days? Let her be shut up for seven days outside the camp, and afterward she may be received again.' So Miriam was shut up outside the camp for seven days, and the people did not move on until Miriam was received again" (Numbers 12:13–15). God didn't only hear the prayers of the patriarchs, but He heard the prayers of kings as well.

Hezekiah is one of my favorite Old Testament kings besides David. His story is evidence of what God will do for those who love Him and call out to Him in their distress. It demonstrates God's mercy, restoration, and blessings.

> 1 In those days Hezekiah became mortally ill. And Isaiah the prophet the son of Amoz came to him and said to him, "Thus says the Lord, 'Set your house in order, for you shall die and not live.' " 2 Then he turned his face to the wall and prayed to the Lord, saying, 3 "Remember now, O LORD, I beseech You, how I have walked before You in truth and with a whole heart and have done what is good in Your sight." And Hezekiah wept bitterly. 4 Before Isaiah had gone out of the middle court, the word of the LORD came to him, saying, 5 "Return and say to Hezekiah the leader of My people, 'Thus says the LORD, the God of your father David, "I have heard your prayer, I have seen your tears; behold, I will heal you. On the third day you shall go up to the house of the LORD. 6 I will add fifteen years to your life, and I will deliver you and this city from the hand of the king of Assyria; and I will defend this city for My own sake and for My servant David's sake." ' " 7 Then Isaiah said, "Take a cake of figs." And they took and laid it on the boil, and he recovered.
>
> 8 Now Hezekiah said to Isaiah, "What will be the sign that the LORD will heal me, and that I shall go up to the house of the LORD the third day?" 9 Isaiah said, "This shall be the sign to you from the LORD, that the LORD will do the thing that He has spoken: shall the shadow go forward ten steps or go back ten steps?" 10 So Hezekiah

> answered, "It is easy for the shadow to decline ten steps; no, but let the shadow turn backward ten steps." 11 Isaiah the prophet cried to the LORD, and He brought the shadow on the stairway back ten steps by which it had gone down on the stairway of Ahaz. (2 Kings 20:1–11)

God also restored people at the request of His prophets, even the unnamed ones. In the next story, the prophet was referred to only as "a man of God" (1 Kings 13:1).

Jeroboam was an evil king who started out following God, but then he did so much evil that the Bible refers to the "sins of Jeroboam" repeatedly. In 1 Kings 13:1–6,[3] King Jeroboam had intended to have this prophet arrested for speaking a word from the Lord. When the king stretched out his hand, it became paralyzed (or "withered," according to one translation), and he could not draw back his hand. "The king cried out to the man of God, 'Please ask the LORD your God to restore my hand again!' So the man of God prayed to the LORD, and the king's hand was restored and he could move it again." If God will heal those who are opposed to Him, how much more should we believe that He will heal us?

Next, in 2 Kings 5 comes the story of a fairly arrogant rich man named Naaman, who was a leper. I love this story because God did more than just heal him, though I am sure that would have been enough. Naaman was commander of the army of the king of Aram, and God had used him to bring a victory in battle. However, he had leprosy. He was a wealthy man, and so he took his chariot and horses and showed up at the prophet Elisha's door. The prophet did not come to meet him but sent a messenger instead, who gave Naaman the prophet's instruction: "Go and wash in the Jordan seven times, and your flesh will be restored to you and you will be clean." Naaman was offended that Elisha didn't even come to the

[3] Bible quotation for this story is taken from the NLT.

door and that he told him to wash in a dirty river instead of some of the cleaner ones Naaman thought would be a better choice. (I believe God chose to humble Naaman.) Naaman was angry until his own servant pointed out his flawed thinking: he was willing to remain sick just because he didn't like the instructions. (Here I would like to point out that offense is what opposes healing.) Verse 14 says, "So he went down and dipped himself seven times in the Jordan, according to the word of the man of God; and his flesh was restored like the flesh of a little child and he was clean." His youth was renewed! What an amazing story that shows God's healing mercy despite our issues.

Another healing story occurs in 1 Kings 17.[4] God used Elijah to bring the widow's child back to life. This widow had been used by God to provide for Elijah. She only had enough oil and flour for one cake, and then she and her son were prepared to die. But then Elijah came, and she fed him first, so God declared, "The bin of flour shall not be used up, nor shall the jar of oil run dry, until the day the LORD sends rain on the earth." Sometime later, after the drought was over, the widow's son became sick and died, so she called for the prophet. "And he stretched himself out on the child three times, and cried out to the LORD and said, 'O LORD my God, I pray, let this child's soul come back to him.' Then the LORD heard the voice of Elijah; and the soul of the child came back to him, and he revived."

The story of the Shunammite woman, also referred to as the notable woman in 2 Kings 4, tells how God restored life to her child through the prophet Elisha. This woman had made a place in her home for Elisha to stay when he came into town, and by doing so she found favor with God, and Elisha prophesied that she would have a child. And so she gave birth to a son, born in her later years. The story tells that the boy grew, and one day he went out to work with his father but started complaining of head pain. His father sent

---

[4] Bible quotations for this story are taken from the NKJV.

him back to his mother, and the servant carried him to her. Then the child collapsed and died in her lap. She took the boy and laid him in the same bed the prophet used. Then she had her servant prepare the donkey and take her to Elisha. Elisha returned to the house and stretched across the child, and life returned to him.

Where It All Began

We can see God's perfect will "in the beginning." Adam and Eve were made in God's image (which means they had the ability to create with their words, but that is another book). Before their bad choice, they lived in harmony with God. The Lord even came and walked with them daily; they had no needs, they were given dominion over the earth and everything in it, and there was no sickness, sorrow, or pain (sounds like heaven, doesn't it?).

I am sure Adam and Eve had knowledge of every plant and its benefits, and this knowledge was passed down from generation to generation because the people originally lived to be nearly a thousand years old. That may be difficult to imagine, but remember we are eternal beings created to spend eternity with God. Later, the lifespan of people continued to get shorter, and then God numbered the days of man at 120 years. God desires that we be healthy, because we cannot fulfill His plan if we are sick or dying. In 3 John 2 (KJV), we read, "Beloved, I wish above all things that thou mayest prosper and be in health, even as thy soul prospereth." Throughout the book of Proverbs, God provides instructions on how to stay in health, and He laid out a detailed plan for health in the Law of Moses.

When we study the Israelites, we can see how God created laws for health and wellness. These laws not only served a spiritual purpose, but they also provided a plan for overall health, prevention of disease, and protection from the spreading of disease. God cares about our health and ultimately desires that we remain well. There are even books that discuss how the biblical laws of food and cleanliness would still work today against sicknesses and diseases.

Under What Conditions?

Under the Law of Moses, otherwise known as the Old Covenant, there were usually conditions attached to healing. Let's take a look at a few of those different scenarios here. We will begin with a Scripture passage that when I read this year, I received a new revelation. Psalm 107 is an amazing psalm that shows the patience and love of God and how far He will go to save us, even from our own messes and from ourselves. God even heals self-inflicted sickness, something I wasn't sure of before, since I thought of those as consequences.

In Psalm 107, four times the Bible tells us, "They cried out to the LORD in their trouble, And He delivered them out of their distresses."[5] Then later we read, "Then they cried out to the LORD in their trouble, And He saved them out of their distresses. He sent His word and healed them, And delivered them from their destructions."[6] God would save the Israelites from their mess, they would worship Him for a while, and then they would fall back into their old ways. They would get into another mess, cry out to God to save them, and He would! I want to point out this also debunks the old saying, "God only helps those who helps themselves!" The only condition we see here was that the Israelites cried out to God after they realized they messed up (again), and He was faithful to come fix it. This happened four times, which means there is no limit on how many times God will help us. On top of that, two more times He not only delivered them from trouble, but He also healed them. Regardless of their repetitive disobedience, God still healed them, because He is a good God. This taught me that God has no limit on

---

[5] See verses 6, 13, 19, 28 NKJV.

[6] See verses 19–20 NKJV.

the number of times I can call on Him for help. It even includes the messes I get myself into. Healing comes not because of who I am, but because of whose I am!

Knowing God will come when we call is not a license to do whatever we want. He is a loving God, and He wants the best for us. We must be wise and seek His guidance in all things. God desires that we live as His children, receiving freely the benefits, the gifts, and the promises He has already provided through Jesus' death and resurrection. Here are a few mores Scripture passages that demonstrate God's will to heal (see Appendix A for additional passages).

"But you shall serve the LORD your God, and He will bless your bread and your water; and I will remove sickness from your midst. There shall be no one miscarrying or barren in your land; I will fulfill the number of your days" (Exodus 23:25–26).

"You shall be blessed above all peoples; there shall not be a male or female barren among you or among your livestock. And the LORD will take away from you all sickness, and will afflict you with none of the terrible diseases of Egypt which you have known, but will lay them on all those who hate you" (Deuteronomy 7:14–15 NKJV).

"Oh, the joys of those who are kind to the poor! The Lord rescues them when they are in trouble. The Lord protects them and keeps them alive. He gives them prosperity in the land and rescues them from their enemies. The Lord nurses them when they are sick and restores them to health" (Psalm 41:1–3 NLT).

"For the LORD God is a sun and shield; The LORD gives grace and glory; No good thing does He withhold from those who walk uprightly" (Psalm 84:11).

"Bless the LORD, O my soul; And all that is within me, bless His holy name! Bless the LORD, O my soul, And forget not all His benefits: Who forgives all your iniquities, Who heals all your diseases, Who redeems your life from destruction, Who crowns you with lovingkindness and tender mercies, Who satisfies your mouth with good things, So that your youth is renewed like the eagle's" (Psalm 103:1–5 NKJV).

How We Are Made

I would like to step out of the Old Testament and talk about the human body. Science works tirelessly to eradicate sickness because the cellular evidence shows that we are created to be continually renewed and therefore should not die. Although much of the how or why within the human body remains a mystery, the medical and scientific communities are still working to discover and unfold these hidden truths. Only the Holy Spirit can reveal these truths because He was present at creation and is present in us today. These truths demonstrate that God's will is to heal the human body.

One definite function of the body that is known in both the medical and scientific communities is that the human body was created to heal itself. This fact alone points to a Creator, but that is a discussion for another day. There are parts of the body that regenerate or create new pathways in response to loss or damage. Even in poor environments with not-so-great nutrition, the body can heal itself, though not as efficiently as when it is provided with the right nutrients and a good environment. Before there was injury, God prepared the body to heal itself.

The human liver is a good example of self-regeneration. A person can be a living donor, which means they are alive and healthy and can donate a portion of their liver to someone in need that meets the matching criteria. Let's say an adult gives a portion of their liver to a child needing a new liver. The liver of the donor (the adult) will grow back within four months, and the liver will return to full function. The child's donated piece will grow as the child grows, and if it is not rejected, it will grow into a full-sized adult liver. However, to prevent (or reduce the risk of) organ rejection, transplant patients must take medications that suppress their immune system for the rest of their lives. This is because the human immune system is designed to fight any and all external invaders, and if left untreated, the immune system will target the new organ as an intruder and attack (reject) it.

Another example of self-regeneration is the heart. After a heart attack, the heart creates what we call collateral vessels that are visible within two weeks. These vessels allow blood flow to go around the area of injury or death to continue feeding other parts of the heart. The human brain similarly creates collateral vessels and new neural pathways after a stroke. Thus, the injured part can see improvement through therapy as it strengthens and creates new pathways. Think of it like supply and demand, except in reverse: because therapy creates a demand on the body part, and the body part is created to work harmoniously within the whole body, new pathways are created to work around the damage. It is quite amazing if you sit and think about it. The alternative is that if you don't create the demand, then the functions of the damaged area and those beyond it are permanently lost.

The statement "Life is in the blood" is true in more than one way. Our blood consists of different types of cells, and if it is missing any of the necessary blood cell categories, our bodies will die. The body makes about two million red blood cells (RBCs) every second, and they have a life span of 120 days in a healthy environment. There are five types of white blood cells (WBCs), and they all work to fight foreign invaders such as bacteria and viruses. (I find this fascinating, but I will restrain myself.) The production of WBCs happens in hours to days, and they have an average life span of one to fifteen days, again depending on the type. The lifespan of platelets, another component of your blood, is seven to ten days, and they have multiple functions in the body. Their main function is to "plug a hole" made in our flesh by an injury. All of this occurs without us even thinking about it, because that is how God created it. As you can see, our blood is being re-created continuously. Our cells are constantly dying and new cells are being created to maintain harmony within the body. If there is any break in this process, we end up at the clinic or the hospital.

Let's consider the parts of the body we can see and actually witness its changes, like the skin. I won't bore you with the details of how the whole body is involved in responding to injury; just remember that platelets are a part of that team. However, the whole process of repairing an injury in our skin can take days or weeks, depending on depth of the injury. The healing time may vary, but functional processes occur with all injuries, both internal and external. We can help the healing process or we can hinder the healing process (leave that scab alone!), but unless we're dead, we cannot stop the healing process! Before there was injury, God prepared the body to heal itself.

CHAPTER 3

Jesus and His Healing Ministry

JOHN G. LAKE reminded the people of his time that Jesus did not heal to persuade the lost to become Christians, He healed because it was His nature! Jesus healed both sinners and saints, both Jews and Gentiles. I confess that in all my years as a follower of God, I had never read the New Testament from start to finish until I enrolled in Bible college. Now, Jesus is my best friend, but previously I had only known Him as my Savior. However, because I thought He was God and not a real man (I will explain more on this later), I couldn't relate to Him or His disciples, so I didn't read much of the New Testament. I have been reading and rereading the Gospels and the book of Acts in addition to my regular Bible reading because I want to know all I can about my Jesus.

My favorite verse in the New Testament (actually the whole Bible) is Acts 10:38, "How God anointed Jesus of Nazareth with the Holy Spirit and with power, who went about doing good and healing all who were oppressed by the devil, for God was with Him" (NKJV). This verse demonstrates to us that Jesus' ministry was done as a man anointed by God, instead of being done by God as a man. I know Jesus wasn't just God pretending to be a man; He was actually a man filled by God. That makes all the difference in believing the ministry of Jesus and God's will to heal today. If it wasn't God's will to heal, then Jesus wouldn't have been doing so much of it. John 5:19 clearly tells us the Father's will to heal. "Therefore Jesus answered and was saying to them, 'Truly, truly, I say to you, the Son can do nothing of Himself, unless it is something He sees the Father doing; for whatever the Father does, these things the Son also does in like manner.' " The moment I understood this truth, it began to dispel one of my biggest wrong beliefs about God, which I will share in detail in a later chapter. What I can tell you is that this revelation had to come from the Holy Spirit, because nothing in my life pointed to it. Without God's help, I could never have comprehended it. The bottom line was that I was deceived, but God has an answer in Scripture for that too!

James 1:16–17 (NKJV) says, "Do not be deceived, my beloved brethren. Every good gift and every perfect gift is from above, and comes down from the Father of lights, with whom there is no variation or shadow of turning." Did you catch that part about "no variation"? That means no changes, and no difference in condition, amount, or level. That tells me that God the Father doesn't change; if He wanted Jesus to go about healing everyone, He still wants that today! I do not know anyone who would consider sickness and disease a "good gift and perfect gift." I know I don't, and neither would those families of my ICU patients who just want their loved ones to live. Let's look at how Jesus handled sickness, disease, and even death.

How Jesus Did It

> "Jesus went about all Galilee, teaching in their synagogues, preaching the gospel of the kingdom, and healing all kinds of sickness and all kinds of disease among the people. Then His fame went throughout all Syria; and they

brought to Him all sick people who were afflicted with various diseases and torments, and those who were demon-possessed, epileptics, and paralytics; and *He healed them*" (Matthew 4:23–24 NKJV).

"Jesus went about all the cities and villages, teaching in their synagogues, preaching the gospel of the kingdom, and *healing every sickness and every disease* among the people" (Matthew 9:35 NKJV).

"Jesus summoned His twelve disciples and gave them authority and power over unclean spirits, to cast them out, and *to heal every kind of disease and every kind of sickness*" (Matthew 10:1 AMP).

"But Jesus, aware of this, withdrew from there. Many followed Him, and *He healed them all*" (Matthew 12:15).

"And when Jesus went out He saw a great multitude; and *He was moved with compassion for them, and healed their sick*" (Matthew 14:14).

"And when the men of that place recognized Him, they sent out into all that surrounding region, brought to Him *all who were sick, and begged Him that they might only touch the hem of His garment. And as many as touched* it *were made perfectly well*" (Matthew 14:35–36 NKJV).

"While the sun was setting, all those who had any who were sick with various diseases brought them to Him; and *laying His hands on each one of them, He was healing them*" (Luke 4:40).

> "And [Jesus] came down with them and stood on a level place with a crowd of His disciples and *a great multitude of people* from all Judea and Jerusalem, and from the seacoast of Tyre and Sidon, who came to *hear him and be healed of their diseases*, as well as those who were tormented with unclean spirits. And they were healed. And the whole multitude sought to touch Him, for power went out from Him and *healed them all*" (Luke 6:17–19 NKJV).

All means *all*! According to *Webster's 1828 Dictionary*, all is "every one, or the whole number of particulars. The whole quantity, extent, duration, amount quality or degree."[7] Even by today's definition, all means "the whole, entire, total, including everything or everyone without exception."[8] Therefore, that should settle the issue in our minds! Unfortunately, it hasn't, and people have taught that the "all" spoken of in the Bible didn't literally mean all. When we start trying to recreate the meanings of words in the Bible, we go down a slippery slope. It means we doubt what the Bible is saying, and that doubt becomes solidified in our minds. If we doubt one part of the Bible, it brings into question the whole Bible, which then undermines our faith in God, and we are unable to receive the promises that belong to us.

As I began studying all the individual healings of Jesus recorded in the Scriptures, I was instructed by God to write them, and so I asked the Holy Spirit to show me what I was missing. This is what I have found so far with the guidance of the Holy Spirit: Many were healed through their faith, most famously the woman with the issue of blood. I also found a few who struggled to believe, two that

---

[7] Noah Webster, *Webster's 1828 Dictionary* (San Francisco, CA: Foundation for American Christian Education), retrieved from https://webstersdictionary1828.com/Dictionary/all.

[8] Merriam-Webster.com Dictionary, s.v. "entire," https://www.merriam-webster.com/dictionary/entire.

did not require their own faith but the faith of others, and one that had no active, or seeking, faith at all. Some were healed through obedience, like the lepers who were told to go and show themselves to the priests. But then there were those who were healed because of Jesus' compassion and a few that Jesus healed to prove a point or because they needed to be free of their bondage. But my favorite discovery (because it showed the humanness of Jesus) was the one healing that did not go as planned. I was shocked too but stick with me; I'll share it and ask the Holy Spirit to reveal it to you.

Healed through Faith

We will begin with the people healed through their own faith. Matthew 9:27–31 tells the story of two blind men following Jesus and crying out for mercy.

> [27] When Jesus departed from there, two blind men followed Him, crying out and saying, "Son of David, have mercy on us!" [28] And when He had come into the house, the blind men came to Him. And Jesus said to them, "Do you believe that I am able to do this?" They said to Him, "Yes, Lord." [29] Then He touched their eyes, saying, "According to your faith let it be to you." (NKJV)

They called Jesus "Son of David," which reveals they recognized Him as the Messiah. They knew His authority. Jesus was saying to them, "You know who I am, but do you know I have the power to heal?" Many believe in who He is, but they don't believe in His power. Their faith in Jesus' power healed them.

One woman with great faith would do anything to be whole, so much so that she spent all her money on physicians, and no one could help her. This is the woman with the issue of blood found in Matthew 9:20–22; Mark 5:25–34; and Luke 8:43–48. She definitely had faith, but how much faith did she have? To answer this, we must know a little about Jewish customs, and for that we can look back at the Law of Moses found in Leviticus.

In Leviticus 15:19–33, we read that a woman who was bleeding was considered unclean, and she would have to remain outside the camp and away from everyone else until her bleeding stopped. Then she would wait seven days before she could return. Upon returning, she had to offer a sacrifice for the priest to purify her before the Lord. Even if her bleeding was not related to her period, as long as she was bleeding, she was ceremonially unclean, and anyone who touched her was considered unclean also. If an unclean person went into town, they had to announce themselves by yelling, "Unclean," repeatedly, so that everyone would stay away.

This woman was bleeding for twelve years. She was isolated, and everyone knew she wasn't allowed in town. She had to break all the Jewish rules, remain covered so no one would recognize her, and start shouting, "Unclean." However, she risked it all because she had made up her mind that this was her day. Jesus was coming, and all she needed to do was reach the edge of His garment—which was breaking another law—and she would be whole.

The Gospel of Luke, my favorite because of the details he gives, tells us that her touch caused the power to go out of Jesus and heal her. She only touched His clothes, not His person, but her faith was so great that it demanded a response! The Greek word for *heal* is from the root *sozo* and indicates that she was made "whole" or "well." *Sozo* means that nothing is missing and nothing is broken. Not only was her bleeding problem healed, but all the mental trauma that went with the disease and the isolation was also healed!

Next, let's consider the story of the paralytic man and his friends, found in Matthew 9:1–8; Mark 2:1–12; and Luke 5:17–26. Jesus was teaching, and the place was packed; even the religious leaders had come from all over. The paralytic man's friends were outside, trying unsuccessfully to get through the crowd. So, his friends climbed up on a roof, tore a hole in it, and lowered the man right in front of Jesus and all those religious leaders.

> 18 Then behold, men brought on a bed a man who
> was paralyzed, whom they sought to bring in and lay
> before Him. 19 And when they could not find how they
> might bring him in, because of the crowd, they went up
> on the housetop and let him down with his bed through
> the tiling into the midst before Jesus. 20 When He saw
> their faith, He said to him, "Man, your sins are forgiven
> you." 21 And the scribes and the Pharisees began to reason,
> saying, "Who is this who speaks blasphemies? Who can
> forgive sins but God alone?" 22 But when Jesus perceived
> their thoughts, He answered and said to them, "Why are
> you reasoning in your hearts? 23 Which is easier, to say,
> 'Your sins are forgiven you,' or to say, 'Rise up and walk'?
> 24 But that you may know that the Son of Man has power
> on earth to forgive sins"—He said to the man who was
> paralyzed, "I say to you, arise, take up your bed, and go to
> your house." 25 Immediately he rose up before them, took
> up what he had been lying on, and departed to his own
> house, glorifying God. (Luke 5:18–25 NKJV)

The paralyzed man's faith is not what brought about his healing; rather, it was the faith of his friends who placed him in front of Jesus, where the healing power of the Lord was present. Luke tells us in verse 17 that the "Pharisees and teachers of the law [were] sitting by, who had come out of every town of Galilee, Judea, and Jerusalem. And the power of the Lord was present to heal them."

Because the religious leaders came with their minds already set against Jesus and what He was doing—that is, they were offended—they missed the power of healing and salvation even though it was there for them. Offense and anger can cause us to miss God, even when He is there for us and His power is in the room.

The story of the centurion's servant, found in Matthew 8:5–13 and Luke 7:1–10, was an example of healing completed through faith, but not the servant's faith. The centurion's servant was sick and about to die, so the centurion asked Jesus to come save the life of his servant. If that was all there was to the story, it would still be a good story; however, Jesus remarked that this Gentile's faith was greater than that of all the Jewish people He had come in contact with. As Matthew gives the account, he says the centurion came to Jesus. Yes, he did, but not in the way we think. Remember that in biblical times, if one sent a representative, it was just as if the person was there. Their representative was them; they were considered the same and had the same authority. Luke gives us a little more detail and tells us that the centurion sent Jewish elders to ask Jesus to come to his home. Then afterward he changed his mind and sent more servants to tell Jesus not to come, because he wasn't worthy for Jesus to come "under [his] roof." The centurion wasn't even the one standing before Jesus at all; it was his representatives! Moreover, Jesus healed the servant from a distance!

At the request of the centurion, Jesus sent His word, and the servant was healed. This references Psalm 107:20 (NKJV): "He sent His word and healed them, And delivered them from their destructions." Not only was the centurion generous and humble, but he also understood the power of authority. He recognized Jesus' authority, and the Bible says, "[Jesus] marveled at him." I want to make Jesus marvel!

Some Faith, Some Doubt

The healing of the leper, found in Matthew 8:1–4; Mark 1:40–45;

and Luke 5:12–15;[9] includes the leper saying, " 'If You are willing, You can make me clean.' Then Jesus, moved with compassion, stretched out His hand and touched him, and said to him, 'I am willing; be cleansed.' As soon as He had spoken, immediately the leprosy left him." Was he unsure about God's will to heal, or was he sure of God's will to heal but unsure of Jesus' authority? We know the leper was Jewish, because according to Matthew 15:24, Jesus answered the Syrophoenician woman, "I was sent only to the lost sheep of the house of Israel." And since the leper was Jewish, he would have known the Torah and known God's compassion on His people. I believe he knew God's will to heal but was unsure of Jesus' authority. Nevertheless, Jesus had compassion and healed him.

Next, let's look at the story of the boy with a demon, found in Matthew 17:14–21; Mark 9:14–29; and Luke 9:37–42.[10] The father of the boy came to Jesus and asked, "If You can do anything, have compassion on us and help us." Jesus said to the father, "If you can believe, all things are possible to him who believes." Then the father cried out, "Lord, I believe; help my unbelief!" and his son was delivered. The father had sought out help from the disciples before coming to Jesus, but they were unable to help. Their failed attempt to heal the boy would have definitely affected the father's trust in Jesus' ability to heal, since He was their rabbi. Nevertheless, Jesus was willing to help his unbelief. I just love Jesus.

Jesus Saw Their Need

The healing of Peter's mother-in-law is found in Matthew 8:14–15; Mark 1:29–31; and Luke 4:38–39. Matthew writes, "When Jesus came into Peter's home, He saw his mother-in-law lying sick in bed with a fever. And He touched her hand, and the fever left her; and

---

[9] Bible quotations for this story are taken from the NKJV.

[10] Bible quotations for this story are taken from the NKJV.

she got up and waited on Him." Jesus saw a need and met it; there is no mention of anyone's faith being required, nor did He command anything from her. The Gospels of Matthew and Mark did not even mention the disciples asking Jesus to heal her. However, Luke's Gospel did say they "besought him" (KJV).

The story of the crippled woman in the synagogue is found in Luke 13:10–17 (not all verses are given below). Jesus was teaching in the synagogue and saw her; then He called her to Him and healed her. There is no mention of faith, except that she was in the synagogue, and no mention of anyone asking (although it was the sabbath, and Jesus addresses that issue later in the story). He saw her need, and He met it.

> [11] And there was a woman who for eighteen years had had a sickness caused by a spirit; and she was bent double, and could not straighten up at all. [12] When Jesus saw her, He called her over and said to her, "Woman, you are freed from your sickness." [13] And He laid His hands on her; and immediately she was made erect again and began glorifying God. (Luke 13:11–13)

After He healed her, we see Jesus give evidence that the devil was responsible for her infirmity in verse 16: "And this woman, a daughter of Abraham as she is, whom satan has bound for eighteen long years, should she not have been released from this bond on the Sabbath day?"

The man with the withered hand is another story of Jesus healing to prove that it was lawful to heal on the Sabbath. This story is found in Matthew 12:9–13; Mark 3:1–5; and Luke 6:6–10. Jesus was in the synagogue, and there sat a man with a withered hand. I have sometimes wondered if God could have planted him there, since the Pharisees were continually trying to catch Jesus doing something they considered unlawful. Again, no mention is made of the man asking for healing, nor does the story mention him having faith, except to obey Jesus' command.

> 6 On another Sabbath He entered the synagogue and was teaching; and there was a man there whose right hand was withered. 7 The scribes and the Pharisees were watching Him closely to see if He healed on the Sabbath, so that they might find reason to accuse Him. 8 But He knew what they were thinking, and He said to the man with the withered hand, "Get up and come forward!" And he got up and came forward. 9 And Jesus said to them, "I ask you, is it lawful to do good or to do harm on the Sabbath, to save a life or to destroy it?" 10 After looking around at them all, He said to him, "Stretch out your hand!" And he did so; and his hand was restored. (Luke 6:6–10)

Through this story, I realized that God is willing to heal diseases that we are willing to live with. This man was in the synagogue, which means he wasn't an outcast; despite his one withered hand, he still was able to earn and provide. Technically, he could live with it because it wasn't going to kill him. However, God doesn't want us living with it; remember the story of the sparrows and the lilies in Matthew 6:25–34 and Luke 12:22–32. How much more important are we to Him!

The healing of the man with dropsy (what we now call *edema*) in Luke 14:1–4 was another healing in which no one asked and no faith was mentioned, but Jesus healed him because the man had a need. Through this healing, Jesus proved that it was lawful to heal on the Sabbath (the religious leaders had a real hang-up with that!).

> 1 It happened that when He went into the house of one of the leaders of the Pharisees on the Sabbath to

> eat bread, they were watching Him closely. [2] And there in front of Him was a man suffering from dropsy. [3] And Jesus answered and spoke to the lawyers and Pharisees, saying, "Is it lawful to heal on the Sabbath, or not?" [4] But they kept silent. And He took hold of him and healed him, and sent him away. (Luke 14:1–4)

I wouldn't mind at all for Jesus to heal me to prove a point.

The story of the high priest's servant is found in Luke 22:49–51. This was the man whose ear Peter cut off with a sword when they were arresting Jesus, just before He was crucified. This man was their enemy; he was there with Judas, the betrayer, to arrest Jesus. But Jesus didn't see His enemy; He saw a man with an immediate need, so Jesus restored his ear. Not only was there no mention of faith from anyone, but it was also an injury, not a disease; it was acute, not chronic; and it was caused by someone else. I point all this out because it changed another wrong idea I had, which was that injuries were not included in sickness and disease. Of course, that was because of my medical science brain, and I did not think it was supported in the Bible (I told you that medical knowledge opposed my faith). Thank God for revelation!

Have Compassion

The man blind from birth, found in John 9, is a long story with many lessons, but my focus will be on the healing, the disciples' question, and Jesus' answer.

The disciples asked Jesus, "Rabbi, who sinned, this man or his parents, that he would be born blind?" Back then, people believed that if someone was born diseased or disabled, then someone had sinned, bringing a curse from God. This teaching was based on the Law of Moses, and until Jesus, those blessings and curses remained in full effect. However, the disciples were more concerned about why he was blind than in healing him, which demonstrated a lack of compassion. Compassion for the hurting and the lost is what will move us into action. Also notice that they even included the man in their question, yet Scripture states he was born blind. Can an infant in the womb sin against God? Therefore, this theology is flawed and is based not on the Law of Moses but on the teachings of the religious leaders of the time. Jesus said that neither had sinned, "but it was so that the works of God might be displayed in him." Jesus spat on the ground, made clay, and put it on the man's eyes. He then told the man, "Go, wash in the pool of Siloam." The man went, washed, and returned healed. Although his blindness was not a result of disobedience or sin, his healing came through his obedience (which in itself is a valuable lesson). For the remainder of the story in verses 8–41, this man was himself persecuted and brought to bear witness about who Jesus was. In this way, he brought glory to God.

Don't Be Satisfied with Less Than Whole

The story of the ten lepers is found in Luke17:11–19. As Jesus was coming into the area, the lepers were off in the distance, yelling for Jesus to have mercy on them. Jesus saw them and commanded them, "Go and show yourselves to the priests." The Bible tells us that as they went, and as they obeyed, they were cleansed. So why does the Bible refer to *cleansing* of lepers but *healing* of sickness and disease? Isn't leprosy a disease? This is where it gets fun—at least for me!

Leprosy actually isn't a disease; it is a type of bacteria that infects the blood. Thus, here we have a blood issue, which according to the Law of Moses would make them unclean. Also, the fact that this illness is caused by bacteria would make them contagious, also rendering them unclean. This particular bacterial blood infection damaged the blood vessels in the body and caused a loss of sensation. We have seen portrayals of lepers with body parts just falling off, but mostly the loss of body parts was due to trauma, having not felt an injury occur. Trauma or injury combined with bacteria would lead to gangrene or necrosis (tissue death), causing it to fall off.

Nine lepers experienced the cleansing of the blood, which meant they could rejoin society. However, that is not the same as healing or restoration. To "cleanse the lepers," or "cleansing" the blood, would only take care of the bacterial infection. From a medical standpoint, the bacteria would be gone, but any external damage or effects could still be seen. So, if they were missing parts, had scars, or suffered from mental trauma from being an outcast, these problems would not have gone away with only a cleansing of the blood unless Jesus restored them.

Of the ten lepers, the Bible tells us that only one returned to Jesus and was restored or made whole (*sozo*) because of his faith. "[Jesus] said unto him, Arise, go thy way: thy faith hath made thee whole" (KJV). All ten had the opportunity for complete restoration but nine were satisfied with less that God's perfect will. Jesus even asked why the other nine didn't return with the one.

Don't Get Robbed of the Promise

The story of the nobleman's son, found in John 4:46–54, gives us some indication on the role of perseverance and not allowing offense. The nobleman was in Cana, where Jesus had turned water into wine, so the man knew of at least one miracle Jesus had performed. He went to ask Jesus to come and heal his son, who was sick and near death. Jesus began by reprimanding the people for not believing in Him without signs and wonders, but the man stayed and interrupted Jesus, pleading for his son's life. The Bible says in verse 50, "Jesus said to him, 'Go; your son lives.' The man believed the word that Jesus spoke to him and started off." Because of this nobleman's faith, not only did he become a believer, but his whole household was saved too! Our belief, or lack of, can change the lives of those around us! How many today would have gone home offended because Jesus did not answer them at first but began preaching about them needing signs and wonders? Had this man not persevered and refused to be offended, his story would have ended very differently.

The story of Jairus' daughter, found in Matthew 9:18–19, 23–26; Mark 5:21–24, 35–43; Luke 8:40–42, 49–56, is an interesting one because right in the middle of his story, another story occurs that changes the story entirely. Jairus's daughter was dying, and as synagogue leader, he had surely heard the stories and even possibly witnessed some of the controversial Sabbath healings. Jesus was surrounded by a large crowd when Jairus came and fell at Jesus' feet. He asked Him to come heal his daughter, and Jesus went. Then the unthinkable happened: the trip was interrupted long enough for Jairus's daughter to die. Why was it interrupted? Because a person with great faith entered the picture. It was here that the woman with the issue of blood touched Jesus and was healed. Jairus was now faced with choices: he had three opportunities we need to consider here. First, Jairus had an opportunity to become offended and blame the woman for his daughter's death. Second, he had the opportunity to celebrate with the woman who received her miracle, while it appeared his daughter would not. Third, He had the opportunity for greater faith and see his daughter raised from the dead. I want to point out that Jairus was a complete contrast to the Pharisees and Sadducees in the way he approached Jesus. Even though Jairus was a leader in the synagogue, he appeared to be a very humble man.

While the commotion of the healing of the woman with the issue of blood was occurring, Jairus's people came and told him his daughter had died. Jesus immediately spoke to Jairus and said, "Do not be afraid; only believe."[11] They arrive at Jairus's house, and the Bible tells us that there was a commotion of loud weeping and wailing.

---

[11] Luke 8:50 NKJV.

As I write this, I can imagine the scene: the mother of the child, the anger, the pain. I can see her husband reassuring her that Jesus is going to fix this and telling her the things that occurred on the way. Then her mourning turns to hope; she can breathe. As she looks into her husband's eyes, she sees calmness and faith. The reason I can so easily see this is because I have watched this scene play out many times in hospitals across the country, and the sound of a mother's wailing is something you never forget.

Back to the story: Jesus verbally declared the girl was not dead but sleeping, and they all began mocking Him. Then Jesus put out all the people who were mourning the daughter and mocking Him. He took her parents and His few chosen disciples, and He entered the room where the child lay. Jesus took her by the hand and said, " 'Talitha kumi!' (which translated means, 'Little girl, I say to you, get up!')" Immediately, she arose and began to walk.

I never knew that the story of the woman with the issue of blood occurred right in the middle of Jairus's story until after my son's death. The first time I saw this, I could feel the offense rising up inside me, because I know how I would have felt and what I would have done in Jairus's situation. I would have been furious with that woman. And when they came and told me my child was dead, I would have went away defeated and angry and preparing to bury a child. I know that, because that is exactly what I did when my son died. It took three years for me to humble myself and come to God for healing. I also had to fight, even after God healed me, to celebrate with other parents whose children received healing while ours did not. I thank the Lord those thoughts no longer occur so I can celebrate and desire healing for others, regardless of my situation. We have choices in our circumstances, and Jairus shows us the right choices.

His Words Never Fail

The healing that did not go as planned was the healing of the deaf-mute man, found in Mark 7:31–37. One morning while studying, I noticed in the passage that Jesus looked up to heaven and sighed. I thought to myself, "That is a strange thing to put in the Bible, unless it is important." So, I pondered it and asked the Holy Spirit to show me why that was worthy of being placed in the Bible. I know He did not put one word in without reason. I double-checked many different translations to be sure it was not a translation issue, and then I looked up the word *sigh* in the dictionary. I could only think that the reason we sigh is in frustration, and surely Jesus wouldn't be frustrated, right? But then I saw it—the Holy Spirit opened my eyes, and my spirit leaped. I knew why He sighed! Then He showed me the issue that caused it, right there in the passage. Let's take a look at the story, and then I will explain more.

> 33 And He took him aside from the multitude, and put His fingers in his ears, and He spat and touched his tongue. 34 Then, looking up to heaven, He sighed, and said to him, "Ephphatha," that is, "Be opened." (Mark 7:33–35 NKJV)

Jesus took him aside, spat, touched his tongue, and placed His fingers in his ears, *but nothing happened!* Then, looking up to heaven, *He sighed and said, "Be opened."* I was shocked. Jesus touched this man, and he wasn't instantly healed? Jesus had the power and authority to heal, but this body did not immediately respond to His authority, and that is the reason He sighed. When I saw this, I realized Jesus was a man, just like us, except He never sinned or made bad choices. Jesus, the Son of God, had just touched a body that didn't respond. Of course He was frustrated.

Then I saw the rest. This is the only recorded healing in which

Jesus had to command the body parts! In all the others, when a command was given, it was for the person to do something, not the parts. He told the man with the withered hand to "stretch out your hand," as opposed to commanding the hand to grow. According to Isaiah 55:11 (NKJV), "So shall My word be that goes forth from My mouth; It shall not return to Me void, but it shall accomplish what I please, And it shall prosper in the thing for which I sent it." The body may not have responded to His touch, but it could not ignore His spoken Word!

Jesus Has Faith When We Don't

The man at the pool of Bethesda was sick for thirty-eight years, as found in John 5:1–15. Jesus went looking for this man; no one asked Him, and no faith was required, which was a good thing because this poor man had lost all hope. When Jesus asked him if he wanted to be healed, the man did not answer the question, but instead he gave all the reasons he wasn't healed. This healing did not come through obedience, because before the man even followed Jesus' command, he was healed. We can see that here in verses 8–9: "Jesus said to him, 'Get up, pick up your pallet and walk.' Immediately the man became well, and picked up his pallet and began to walk."

When I mention "no faith," I am talking about active, seeking faith. There are different levels of faith, and only God knows our hearts and where our faith level actually is. As we have seen, healing does come through faith, but there are healings that occurred without an overcoming faith, and this should give us all hope. I pray that we can see and feel God's love and care for us and how He truly desires we be in health in all areas of our lives. I hope we are beginning to dispel the lies of the enemy concerning healing and now have more evidence for God's will to heal.

CHAPTER 4

Err on the Side of Jesus

FOR DECADES, I have watched countless people request prayer for healing, only for someone tell them, "I will pray with you, but you know Jesus didn't heal everyone." I have also been that person, until something inside me rose up, and I realized we have an error in our thinking concerning healing. Somewhat similar to having a blind spot in a car, we can see almost everything, but there is one place we cannot see. We have been so quick to focus on what Jesus didn't do, instead of focusing on what He did do, that we even find Scripture passages to support our view. We have erred on the side of doubt about healing for decades and have made statements that are contrary to what the Bible tells us, contrary to God's heart. This has to stop! We must become defenders of our faith. If we err, we should do so on the side of Jesus. The Holy Spirit is the one who can reveal our blind spot(s). The light He shone on my blind spots has changed my thinking, praying, and living. This is going to be a journey, so stick with me.

As evidenced in the previous chapter, the Bible tells us Jesus healed "all," and the only requirements for most of these were that the people came, sought, asked, or expected to be healed (see the different levels of faith here). We also saw that Jesus healed out of compassion. Does this mean Jesus miraculously healed or restored everyone? No. Remember the story of the ten lepers? Only one was completely restored. There is a difference between healing, restoration, and miracle (we will define these later). While this may seem like splitting hairs, this is a subject that definitely needs splitting, and the Holy Spirit knows just how to do it. Hebrews 4:12 (NLT) says, "For the word of God is alive and powerful. It is sharper than the sharpest two-edged sword, cutting between soul and spirit, between joint and marrow. It exposes our innermost thoughts and desires." We are going to take a moment here and dig deeper to gain understanding, because without it the enemy deceives us.

Seeds of Doubt

The enemy has gotten away with these tactics too long, and it is time to correct our errors. I am angry at the doubt, the lies, and the enemy who creates them, just like he did in the Garden. Notice what he said to Eve in Genesis 3:1: "Did God really say," or "Did God actually say," or even, "Has God indeed said." Then in the New Testament, he attempted the same trick with Jesus: "If You are the Son of God . . ."[12] Of course, Jesus didn't buy it. No matter which translation we use, the bottom line is that satan plants *seeds of doubt*. He did it with Eve, and he is still doing that same thing today.

If the enemy can introduce one seed of doubt, then without God's word, or *rhema*, that seed will take root, grow, and choke out the truth or prevent truth from taking root. Before we go any further, let's define these two Greek words, *logos* and *rhema*. Both are referred to in the New Testament and translated as "word" in the English language (a perfect example of why we need to study the Bible more closely). *Logos,* G-3056 in Strong's, is used 331 times in the New Testament. It is defined as "something said [notice the past tense], the expression of thought, reasoning, or an account" (not provided here are the terms for Jesus as the living Logos). It refers

[12] Matthew 4:3 NKJV.

to the written Word of God, the Holy-Spirit-inspired Scriptures. *Rhema*, G-4487 in Strong's, is used 59 times in the New Testament. It is defined as an "utterance, a command, instruction, or a saying (present tense)." It is the spoken word of God, a direct word from God given to us by the Holy Spirit that confirms His written Word. It is what we refer to as "a revelation from God." If we have *logos* without *rhema*, the Bible becomes just another history book. If we have *rhema* without *logos*, we cannot test the spirits, according to 1 John 4:1, to know if the instruction received is from God.

Now let's discuss the difference in our earthly lives using Adam and Eve as our example. Genesis 2:16–17 tells how God told Adam the rules of the Garden. Adam heard the rules directly from God; this is *rhema*. Notice Eve had not been created yet, so Adam had to pass on to Eve the instructions God had said. Eve heard from the man, making this *logos* for her, because she did not hear it directly from God.

There they were in the Garden of Eden (a perfect environment), and it only took one seed of doubt spoken by the enemy for Eve to abandon the *logos* truth. She went from living with God to sinning against God. Adam, on the other hand, had *rhema*, and he chose to eat of the fruit. Therefore, he disobeyed the command of God and chose Eve over God (that in itself was a sin also).

A seed of doubt is the same thing the judicial system calls "reasonable doubt," which is just enough to throw out all the proven evidence of the case. Most of the definitions I came across for the word *reasonable* mentioned the word or its root word in the definition, which I do not find very helpful. So instead, let's look at the root word *reason* in *Webster's 1828 Dictionary*. "Reason: That which is thought or which is alleged in words, as the ground or cause of opinion, conclusion, or determination."[13]

The enemy uses our thoughts against us. Moreover, he plants

[13] Noah Webster, *Webster's 1828 Dictionary* (San Francisco, CA: Foundation for American Christian Education), retrieved from https://webstersdictionary1828.com/Dictionary/all.

his thoughts in our minds, making us believe they are ours. If we accept them or act upon them, he wins that area. Many times, we cannot tell the difference between our thoughts and the enemy's, because man is not a good judge of thoughts. Now let's look to the Bible to see what God says about our reason or thoughts. According to Proverbs 14:12, "There is a way which seems right to a person, But its end is the way of death."

> "'For My thoughts are not your thoughts, Nor are your ways My ways,' declares the LORD. 'For as the heavens are higher than the earth, So are My ways higher than your ways and My thoughts than your thoughts' " (Isaiah 55:8–9).

> "And now, dear brothers and sisters, one final thing. Fix your thoughts on what is true, and honorable, and right, and pure, and lovely, and admirable. Think about things that are excellent and worthy of praise" (Philippians 4:8 NLT).

> "For who knows a person's thoughts except the spirit of that person, which is in him? So also no one comprehends the thoughts of God except the Spirit of God" (1 Corinthians 2:11 ESV).

> "Let no man deceive himself. If any man among you thinks that he is wise in this age, he must become foolish, so that he may become wise" (1 Corinthians 3:18).

> "For as he thinks within himself, so he is. He says to you, 'Eat and drink!' But his heart is not with you" (Proverbs 23:7).

These Scripture passages show us that our natural thinking is flawed, influenced by man's sinful nature, the enemy, and this world.

Therefore, it will not help in understanding the things of God; we need the Holy Spirit to provide understanding and discernment. Previously, the enemy had used my thoughts to believe the lie that Jesus didn't heal all, despite the Word saying He did. There are two specific instances of Jesus' ministry that many sermons have discussed to show how Jesus didn't heal all and that therefore God doesn't heal all. This sows seeds of doubt and unbelief about healing, God, and His Word.

The Scripture passages that are most often used by the enemy to create a reasonable doubt about Jesus (yes, the enemy knows and uses the Scriptures) are found in Mark 6:1–6 (specifically verses 5–6) and John 5:2–15. Since this did not line up with what I knew about God's heart toward us, as I read these Scripture passages, I prayed and asked for guidance from God concerning them. Then I began studying these Scripture passages word by word through various translations, Strong's, and most importantly, the guidance of the Holy Spirit. What He revealed has transformed my thinking, and I want to ask the Holy Spirit to give understanding to all who read this.

Jesus in Nazareth

I began to read Mark 6:5 again, and I caught the second half this time: "Now He could do no mighty work there, except that He laid His hands on a few sick people and healed them."[14] We easily latch onto the first half of that verse, but we ignore the second half. We had taken the first part and jumped to verse 6, how Jesus marveled at their unbelief, and we concluded that Jesus couldn't heal because of unbelief. Yes, unbelief is in direct opposition to healing, but what about Jesus' healings of compassion, the healings that didn't require active faith, and the testimony of Acts 10:38? There has to be more to this we haven't seen.

---

[14] Mark 6:5 NKJV.

At the beginning of Mark 6, Jesus was teaching in the synagogue, and many who heard Him were astonished by His wisdom. However, the very next verse says they were offended at Him. We could stop and say, "There it is—they weren't healed because of their offense." Yes, we know that offense is a tool the enemy used to rob us of the promises of God, but that doesn't tell the whole story either. That only includes the ones in the synagogue, the religious leaders, and their followers. What about the other people? We know that according to Acts 10:38, Jesus "went about doing good and healing all who were oppressed by the devil."

What about the "mighty work" mentioned in verse 5, or that fact that He did heal a few in Nazareth? Follow me here, as we are going to define a few words before I provide the concluding thoughts on Mark 6:5–6. According to Strong's, the words *mighty* and *work* have the same meaning. Both are taken from the same Greek word, G-1411, *dunamis*, meaning "miracles, miraculous power, virtue, or work." According to this definition, Jesus, while in Nazareth, could do no miracles, had no miraculous power, and no virtue went out of Him in Nazareth. Some translations say, "He could do no miracle." The definition of *miracle* is "extraordinary event, beyond all natural laws, beyond all human ability."

Most of us would consider healing a miracle, but it is mentioned separately from mighty works and miracles in Mark 6:5. It is also implied in Mark 6:2, when they people in the synagogue of Nazareth were shocked at Jesus' wisdom and understanding. They even say toward the end of verse 2, "and such miracles as these performed by His hands." Look again at verse 5, where He could do no miracles except healing a few sick. Healing is also not listed as a mighty work in Strong's, so let's define the word *healing*. *Healing* is "a process of making or becoming healthy again, a gradual process through the regeneration of cells." We spoke earlier about how God created the body to heal itself; by definition, healing can occur without it being a miracle. I am unsure if God considers healing a miracle or how these people were healed. John G. Lake says it this way: "Healing is the renewal of the body from diseased conditions. A miracle is in the creative order."[15] In Hebrews 6:1, the author refers to raising the dead as a foundational doctrine, so it is possible that God's definition differs from ours (His thoughts are higher than ours). However, not knowing the answer does not negate the healings that took place. "Now He could do no mighty work [miracle] there, except that He laid His hands on a few sick people and healed them."

Jesus healed all who came, sought, or believed for healing. The people of Nazareth clearly lacked faith and belief, but some came to be healed. I believe more people did not seek Him for healing because they had seen Him grow up as a normal Jewish boy, and they were struggling with who He was. A spirit of familiarity stands in direct opposition to the anointing of God. Because they thought they knew Him, they became offended, and we will not seek what we believe we already know or that which offends us.

In 2 Timothy 3:16 (NKJV), the Bible says, "All Scripture is given by inspiration of God, and is profitable for doctrine, for reproof, for correction, for instruction in righteousness." Therefore, in accordance with James 1:16–17; Matthew 4:23–24; Matthew 9:5; Matthew 14:14; Luke 4:40; and Acts 10:38, I believe that Jesus did indeed heal all who came to Him in Nazareth. The key is that there were few who came or sought Him out, according to Scripture, because He was familiar to them. We must be careful what we are familiar with; God may be trying to bring us to deeper truths, but we won't receive them if we think we already know them.

The Pool of Bethesda

The second story satan uses to create doubt about healing is found

---

[15] John G. Lake, quoted in Roberts Liardon, ed., *The Collected Works of John G. Lake*, (Tulsa, OK: Albury Publishing, 1999), 492. Used by Permission.

in John 5:2–15. The Bible only mentions one man at the pool that Jesus heals. This is the main text used by Christians, even by some who have had healing ministries, to say God doesn't heal all. It is the one I believed until I met the real Jesus, not just the one I had been taught. To think He only healed one in a place where thousands lay sick goes against His character. I just cannot see Jesus stepping over sick and dying people, who could have been grabbing at Him or at His clothes, to go and heal just one man. Not after all the other stories of compassion, and how He would stop and care for their needs. No, I don't think that's all He did there, and here are my thoughts and my evidence.

> [2] Now there is in Jerusalem by the Sheep Gate a pool,
> which is called in Hebrew, Bethesda, having five porch-
> es. [3] In these lay a great multitude of sick people, blind,
> lame, paralyzed, waiting for the moving of the water. [4] For
> an angel went down at a certain time into the pool and
> stirred up the water; then whoever stepped in first, after
> the stirring of the water, was made well of whatever dis-
> ease he had. [5] Now a certain man was there who had an
> infirmity thirty-eight years. (John 5:2–5 NKJV)

According to Nehemiah 3:1, the Sheep Gate was a part of the wall of Jerusalem, and it was the northern gate. This gate was used to bring the sheep through that would be used for temple sacrifices. Near this gate was a pool called Bethesda, which means "house of mercy" or "house of grace." Surrounding the pool were five porches (some translations call them *colonnades*, which is a row of columns supporting a roof). In those porches lay a great multitude. A *multitude* typically meant thousands, and remember, only men were counted. The location, the name, and the sick people present set the stage for something huge and supernatural. I cannot help but feel there is so much more to this story than we have recognized.

Could other miracles have occurred there and not been recorded? Yes, John 20:30 (NLT) tells us, "The disciples saw Jesus do many other miraculous signs in addition to the ones recorded in this book." Yes, you know I am going to say it: Acts 10:38 (NKJV) tells us "how God anointed Jesus of Nazareth with the Holy Spirit and with power, who went about doing good and *healing all* who were oppressed by the devil, for God was with Him." We have already established that sickness and disease do not come from God, according to James 1:16–17. We have also established God's will to heal; for that list of Scripture passages, see Appendix A. Those verses alone should be enough to convince us there's more to this story that we don't know. While the Bible does not tell us that He healed all the people at the pool, it also doesn't say He didn't; in fact, it just doesn't mention them after the opening scene was set.

I propose that the reason the Bible only recorded the one healing was because the man had been there thirty-eight years, making him a special case. He tells Jesus of the people who stepped over him and got in the water first. The Bible says, "When Jesus saw him lying there, and knew that he already had been in that condition a long time." Just how many people did that man watch come and go while he sat there? Now he was disappointed, beaten down, and without hope; he had given up. He even made excuses to Jesus why he wasn't healed. "Sir, I have no man to put me into the pool when the water is stirred up; but while I am coming, another steps down before me." This man had no faith (what faith he had years ago was gone); he barely even had hope. He was so dejected that all he had were excuses why he was still there.

This healing should give us all hope. It means there's hope for those who have lost all hope when Jesus has compassion and comes on the scene. I believe the reason this man's story is the only one recorded at the pool of Bethesda is because it is a case of precedence, the law of first mention (we will talk more about that later).

For now, let's go back and reset the scene: near the northern gate of the wall of Jerusalem, there was a pool called the "house of mercy" or "house of grace." Beside it lay thousands of sick people, blind, lame, and paralyzed, hoping to be healed. We know that hope isn't the same as faith, but hadn't they taken some action with their hope? They weren't at home hoping, or somewhere else in Jerusalem hoping; they were there, waiting near the water that an angel would stir on occasion. According to Strong's, G-1551, *ekdechomai*, "waiting," also means "expecting, look for, tarry, to take or rescue from, to await." Are these not some of the same terms that are used when talking about faith?

I was thinking about how Jesus walked onto that scene. Did He go straight to the man and heal him first, or did He heal others and then the man? Then as I wrote and pondered, I felt the Holy Spirit sharing things I had never considered before. The pool was at the Sheep Gate; according to John 10, Jesus is the Good Shepherd. John also speaks of Jesus as the door (John 10:9), and those who find Him will go in and out freely to pasture. According to Jeremiah 2:13; 17:13, the prophet describes God as "the fountain of living water[s]." In John 4:10, Jesus is the living water. These people were waiting by both the Sheep Gate and the water in a place called "mercy" or "grace."

Since the other people in the porches were waiting or expecting, they had hope and, by evidence of their actions, some level of faith. Although their faith was misguided, looking to angels and a pool for healing, Jesus could not ignore it. Jesus went to the man first, then as the others heard or saw what happened, their faith grew. The whole place was stirred, and virtue went out of Jesus and healed them all. I also thought of how Peter's shadow healed the sick; how did those people know to lay their sick along Peter's path? Had they heard a story; did Jesus have that happen here first? I will be asking God about it when I get to heaven or when I see Him.

No matter how it occurred, because we are not told, I have to look to Scripture and know that there are no accidents or coincidences in the Bible. The Hebrew language is beautifully complex, and the meanings of its letters and words are very intentional. Everything points to Jesus healing *all* at the pool of Bethesda! These people were waiting for a stirring of the waters, and then Jesus, the Living Water, walks on the scene. That is not a coincidence!

The enemy wants me to believe that God left all those people expecting to be healed, waiting around a pool that an angel stirred, where only one was healed each time. Not my God!

The enemy wants me to believe that the Good Shepherd, the Door to Life, walked onto the scene of the porches at the Sheep Gate, and He only led one out? Not my God!

The enemy wants me to believe that my Jesus walked by all of those sick and dying people who were desperate, hoping, putting what little faith they had in water that wasn't alive, and when the Living Water walked onto the scene, He healed one and walked away? Not my God!

The enemy wants me to believe that Jesus, by healing only one, did no greater work than an angel stirring the water. Not my God!

How can I believe something that speaks against what my God, Jesus, the Holy Spirit, and the Scriptures themselves declare, when there is so much evidence of His goodness, mercy, and grace? The Word repeatedly tells us that He healed them all; therefore, in accordance with all the aforementioned Scripture passages, I believe without a shadow of a doubt that Jesus did heal all. I do not know why the Bible does not tell of these people being healed; maybe it was because there were so many that the disciples couldn't keep up with the recording. Maybe it was because those healings were done through faith, and there were already examples the Holy Spirit had given for this. Maybe since the healing of multitudes though His virtue was already recorded four times He did not think it necessary to tell another like it.

Maybe it is a test of our faith, our trust in Him, to see who would believe against all odds in the goodness of God and His desire to heal all. He tested His disciples repeatedly, and He desires that we have faith and trust His heart, just as He expected them to have. No matter the reason that the rest of the healings aren't recorded, we must take what the Scriptures do say and apply it to all similar situations.

> "Now faith is the substance of things hoped for, the evidence of things not seen" (Hebrews 11:1 NKJV).

> "Now to Him who is able to do far more abundantly beyond all that we ask or think, according to the power that works within us" (Ephesians 3:20).

> "For I am persuaded that neither death nor life, nor angels nor principalities nor powers, nor things present nor things to come, nor height nor depth, nor any other created thing, shall be able to separate us from the love of God which is in Christ Jesus our Lord" (Romans 8:38–39 NKJV).

Remember, even though they were in a perfect environment (the Garden), humans bought the lies of the enemy and gave in to the seed of doubt. Now, our environment is a sin-entangled world and the lies of the enemy are everywhere, which is why God gives us directions in His Word. He instructs us to guard our hearts, to think on good (godly) things, and to meditate on His Word day and night. Then He sent Jesus to earth as a man anointed by God, who is our example of how to overcome the enemy and the seeds of doubt. Finally (but not last), God sent His Holy Spirit to guide us and to bring us *rhema* as we travel the earth. What I have seen, I cannot unsee; what I have heard, I cannot unhear, and no one will convince me otherwise. I pray that the Holy Spirit gives everyone who reads this eyes to see, ears to hear, and a heart of understanding.

CHAPTER 5

Personal Healing Testimonies

FOR MANY YEARS, I had read about the numerous miraculous healings surrounding the Generals of the faith. Then I stopped reading them, thinking I knew this part of God (but remember how Jesus could do little in His hometown because they knew Him). It wasn't until I showed up at the revival in Dawsonville that I realized I had put those things out of my mind because I didn't want to experience any disappointment. However, hearing, seeing, and reading testimonies of healing, provision, debt cancellation, and some things we can barely imagine, helps us grow in our own faith. (The enemy knows that.)

Revelation 12:11 tells us that we overcome the enemy by the blood of Jesus and the word of our testimony. If you don't know what your testimony is, then speak what the Word says about you and make that your testimony (that should actually be the base of all of our testimony). Pray and ask God to reveal your testimony to you; sometimes it is there but we just don't realize it.

Testimonies of God working in the lives of others are not something to be jealous or angry about; they are to be celebrated, because what He did it for one, He will do it for any. I do not throw around the word *miracle* lightly; I was actually convicted by the Holy Spirit a few years back for using the term in everyday language, because it was creating expectations. Let us define again what a *miracle* is.

From the modern dictionary: "an extraordinary event, beyond all natural laws, beyond all human ability." In Strong's, G-1411-*dunamis,* always points to a new or higher forces that have entered and are working in our lower world, or power in action; H-4159 is a divine act or special display of power outside the realm of ordinary providence; H-6381 indicates something to be marvelous, extraordinary, beyond one's power to do, or actions beyond human power.

While there have been a few miracles in my life, there have been more interventions, blessings, and moments of God keeping me here so I can fulfill His calling. The enemy has attempted to end my life more than once, but God has brought the right people at the right times to walk me through it. God has supernaturally touched me and even encouraged my high expectations of Him.

Since my childhood, I have been in awe of God and His power being manifested on the earth. Ephesians 3:20 (NKJV) says, "Now to Him who is able to do exceedingly, abundantly above all that we ask or think, according to the power that works in us." I love this verse because it taught me that the one who gave me my imagination and these expectations can (and will) do more even than that! However, for many years, because my imagination is so wild, I struggled with that verse. I openly doubted, though I still hoped. I would warn God, "Okay, but I can dream or imagine some pretty big stuff." This opened an unknown door for the enemy to use my imagination and expectations to create disappointment, first in myself and later in God.

I was the child that would believe against all odds that my God will work. I would have been one of the children at the Red Sea, telling the adults to just wait, expecting to see God either move the water or transport us to the other side. I was a dreamer among dreamers, but that isn't always encouraged by people! However, God is the author of dreams. God tells us in Matthew 18:3 that we must come as little children if we are to enter the kingdom of God (and He isn't talking about heaven here). Children have big imaginations and dreams. They believe anything you tell them, and they are full of faith—until they grow up and begin to doubt.

My expectations create excitement because I know who God is, who I am in Him, and that He gave me this mind for a reason. Those expectations kept me hoping in God, despite all the ways the enemy was trying to attack me, because He had buried something deep inside me that longed to see Him move. That longing is why I love the Old Testament so much: it tells hundreds of stories of how God took ordinary, messed up people and then blessed them, used them, supernaturally delivered them (many times), and showed them signs to prove Himself.

I began to learn and read about miracles in which body parts were restored, surgically placed metal plates or parts came out of people, weight loss occurred instantly, or cancer masses fell out onto the floor. Not all of these occurred in the presence of someone praying for them; some of these miracles occurred while the person was listening to the radio, watching television, driving, or even while he or she was sleeping. These documented miracles range in dates from the 1600s until the late 1980s, and even my mind and imagination have trouble comprehending some of them. I ponder these miracles often because of my medical background and my dislike of the sounds bones make when moving (to the point I almost passed out in the ER one day). Some of these miracles even disturb me while creating awe, because when someone is dead with their head on backward, to be honest, I am probably going to leave them there and help other injured people.

I ask God to give me eyes to see Him working against my medical knowledge, a heart to follow His Spirit no matter how it appears, and ears to hear Him as clearly as the people did when they saw the woman whose neck was internally severed in a wreck (mentioned above). The main thing about hearing or reading about these miracles is to sit and think about them, compare them to the works of Jesus and the apostles, and realize, as the Bible says in Luke 1:37, that nothing is impossible with God! I believe that soon we will walk in the commission of Matthew 10:8, but until then I sit and learn all I can from the Holy Spirit and from those Christians who have participated in the miraculous.

I have immersed myself in the Word and read the teachings of the Generals, and I can see a shift happening in my thinking. The Holy Spirit is able to show me where I missed His message, or where I am missing it, and what areas I need to work on. The most recent revelation was that if we doubt any area of the Bible, that gives the opportunity for the enemy to create doubt in other areas of the Word. This explains why we believe in salvation but struggle to believe in healing, or how we can believe in healing but struggle with believing in provision. Jesus paid for them all! It is the divine exchange; it is the covenant; it is salvation. I have shared the story of God's intervention at my birth, and now I want to share more stories of God's healing power in and through my life.

Sometimes Ignorance Denies Opportunity for Doubt

During my first pregnancy, God intervened a few times. I was four months pregnant when I went to the doctor for the first time. Let me explain; my new, also young, husband was in the Army, and we had no clue how to use the medical system. However, my mom kept close watch on me, and after all, I was young and healthy, so we weren't too concerned. Then one morning I couldn't catch my breath, and I had this rash all over me. My mom immediately recognized it as chicken pox, so she called the base hospital, and they told us to get there immediately, as chicken pox creates a very high risk for miscarriage. When we arrived, we discovered the reason I couldn't breathe wasn't the chicken pox, but it was that my heart rate was at 174 bpm. The doctors immediately began treating me. I was placed in isolation due to the virus and monitored because of risk of miscarriage. Because of my young age and the new onset of a rapid heart rate, it was now considered a high-risk pregnancy. But God intervened, and all the chicken pox spots were dried up and gone completely within four days. I did not miscarry this time, nor later following the amniocentesis (a procedure in which a long needle is stuck in through your abdomen to get a sample of fluid around the baby). Because of the high risk, I had multiple ultrasounds, and around six months, one of them showed a large mass on my ovary that wasn't there previously. Mom called her brother, and again half of Georgia and Texas were praying, and at the repeat ultrasound the mass was gone. I want to say here that ignorance does help sometimes, because I was clueless and had no thoughts about cancer or anything being wrong, so there was no opportunity for doubt or fear to attack my thoughts. I was hospitalized multiple times during this pregnancy. I had UTIs repeatedly (which are another risk for miscarriage), and during the last weeks I was kept in the hospital until the baby was born. I can trace accounts of doctors being moved around on my behalf, the cardiologist intervening to prevent harm to me and the baby, and then, when the spinal block went horribly wrong and I was paralyzed (temporarily) from the nose down, I saw God's hand again. Baby and I came home from the hospital sixteen days after my final admission, both happy and healthy.

It was at this moment that postpartum depression (PPD) took a huge toll on me. Between that, the weight I had gained, and a baby that seemed to never sleep, I was a mess. This happened before anyone really knew to screen for PPD. I would call my mom and tell her how I felt, and she would tell me to pray and that it would get better. This was how she had gotten through everything, and it was all she knew to do. This went on for over eighteen months and was compounded with my childhood trauma; however, yet again I told no one. It was so bad that when my husband was gone for military training, I would put water and bread on the table where my toddler could reach it, or I make sure he had a clear climbing path to the table in case I died and no one knew we were there. My fear of being alone and of everyone around me dying had transferred to a fear of me dying and leaving my baby alone. I can tell you that from a medical professional standpoint, a mental health standpoint, and a spiritual standpoint, there is no other reason I survived such deep depression without help, except for God keeping me. There was nothing I did; I was not a person who would pray for hours. I only survived because of God's love (and He loves and cares for us all).

Shortly after the PPD had improved, I was pregnant with our second child, which was a complete shock because I was on the pill and had never missed a day. Thankfully, this pregnancy did not have all the internal complications of the first. I was already on medication to control my heart rate; it only needed to be changed to a different one. Again, I was placed on high-risk precautions with regular ultrasounds, but they showed nothing but the baby. However, this delivery was an issue, not for Christopher, but for me.

I do want to back up for a moment and tell you how the enemy had been after this child since the beginning, but God kept him tucked safely inside of me (I'll discuss it more in chapter 7). A few events occurred during this pregnancy that could have caused a miscarriage for sure: I was involved in two car wrecks for which I was not at fault. However, the main event happened one winter day when I slipped on some ice, fell down the brick stairs, and landed hard on my backside. As I was falling, I reached out to grab something to steady myself, and a wheelbarrow of firewood fell on top of my belly. At that moment, I became aware that the enemy was trying to kill this child and maybe me in the process. However, God had us covered (most likely due to my mom's many prayers, as I wasn't following the Lord closely at the time).

Aside from those trips to the hospital to be monitored, nine months flew by this time around. The day came for delivery. I had not slept all night because they admitted me the day prior and had put in an IV that was the size of a garden hose and my arm hurt.

(IVs are an issue in the family, and this is why I became a specialist in starting them as a nurse.) However, I was thankful for it because I was going to need it. The spinal block went well this time. It was a little bit into the surgery; I felt a little pressure and a few tugs, and I heard the doctor say, "Mrs. *(Name)*, you're doing great." In the very same moment, they called for the crash cart. They were losing me and lying to me about it. As they pushed drugs to get my heart under control, I began to pray and remain calm. They then discovered that I had a mass on my right ovary (again) that weighed ten pounds and was the size of a grapefruit. Again, I never once considered that it could be cancer or feared anything bad, but it did take so long for them to get it out that the spinal block was wearing off, and I could feel the pinch of the sutures and every bit of the staples. Lying flat for the next eight hours was torture because I could move my body normally and I was ready to get up and go. I felt great, despite all the things that had occurred in the operating room. For those in suspense, the tumor was benign, but the recovery at home was rough. I had felt so good at the hospital that I refused any pain medication for home.

Same Issues, Different Ways to Healing

In 1997, I was in charge of the plane crash scene for Tribulation Trail, an event about the end times we did at my church every October. This particular year it was unusually cold, so we were standing around in our costumes drinking hot cocoa when we heard a group coming. We all quickly took our places among the "dead." I happened to lie right across an exposed tree root. I was unable to move and had to remain perfectly still (we took our acting seriously). When I started to get up, my back was very tender, so I waited and expected it to go away. Instead, it got worse. Our pastor (a neighbor and friend) came by and ended up taking me back to the church in the golf cart. He instructed me to go to the hospital because by now

I could barely walk and was holding my breath from the pain. I told him I didn't need a hospital; I just wanted to call my mom so she could lay hands on me, and I would be healed. This was a Baptist church, and though we were a little freer than the one I grew up in, he still looked at me kind of funny and shook his head. (He already thought I was nuts because I was seeking the baptism of the Holy Spirit, and he disapproved.) We couldn't locate my mom, and it was really late at night, so they sent me to the hospital anyway (most likely for insurance purposes).

I arrived at the ER in my costume, appearing like I had just been burned in a plane crash. I had to calm down the person at the front desk and tell her where I was coming from. She just shook her head (everyone in the area was familiar with our event). It turned out I didn't have any disc or spinal cord injury, only a very bad muscle spasm of one of the larger back muscles. They drugged me up and sent me home on bed rest. I was sleeping on the couch (it was firmer than our bed) and taking anti-inflammatory medications, muscle relaxers, and pain pills every four to six hours. I slept almost around the clock and was a zombie for almost five days. Finally, I realized I needed to do something different. I could still barely move; nothing was helping, and when I stopped taking those medications, I had a horrible mental battle. I called my mom to come get me, and she took me to her church. I literally crawled hands and knees down the aisle at the Pentecostal church my mom had been attending. I had brought a couple pillows, and I laid myself at the altar through the whole service. I told the Lord (and the pastor) that I wasn't leaving until I was healed and could walk out! A few hours later, I walked out with my back healed and free from the side effects of the medications. Following this episode, I began going to this church with mom, and for the next few years life was amazing. I was walking in the continual presence of the Holy Spirit like I had never known before. However, in 1998, my lack of knowledge and understanding of God the Holy Spirit resulted in this gift going dormant for many years.

Shifting Bones and Disobedience

This healing was nothing short of a miracle that happened in the early 2000s. I would learn lessons in obedience, that delayed obedience was still disobedience, and that disobedience has consequences (not from God, but it allows the enemy room to work). According to 1 Samuel 15:22, obedience is better than sacrifice. I want to share here an analogy my mom gave when explaining to me how disobedience allows the enemy access to us. Picture God's protection like a large umbrella He is holding over us. As long as we remain with Him, walking with Him and under His protection, then the enemy has no access to us. However, if we do not remain under His protection by failing to follow His guidance, or if we leave the safety of His protection though disobedience, then we are outside of His covering, and the enemy can have access to us. Psalm 91 talks of all the things that will occur around us but not come near us if we abide in Him. I also want to point out that life around us is not free of trouble even under divine protection. It is through the Holy Spirit that we will discern issues of life versus the attack of the enemy (this is where much confusion lies).

One Wednesday night, the boys and I were at church when someone came from the youth building to the choir room to tell me my son had broken his foot. On my way to the youth building, I heard very clearly the Lord telling me to lay hands on his foot, and it would be healed. When I arrived, I could see the bone protruding just under the skin, clearly broken. I was too embarrassed to pray with all those people around me. I was more afraid of what people would think than of what God had said. So, I decided to do the next best thing instead, which sounded good to my religious spirit. I would take my son home, and Mike and I would lay hands on him and believe together as his parents. However, that was not what God had said. The Lord knew that this miracle would have built up faith in Mike, the boys, and myself, as well as the others who were standing around. I was told to pray right there on the steps of the church building with all those people watching. As I write this, it hurts my heart to remember and to know only some of the cost my disobedience.

I went home, and Mike had me take Joshua to the ER. On our way, I called my mom and told her all that happened, and I asked her to come pray with me. God in His graciousness moved on our behalf. Mom and I had Joshua's leg and foot in our hands. As we began to pray, we heard bones popping, the foot moving, and Joshua hollering. We opened our eyes and took our hands off to see that the bone had gone back into place. At this point, we should have kept praying, but we were so shocked that our prayers actually worked (shame on us for being surprised) that we stopped praying. We took Joshua into the ER for X-rays, fully expecting them to say nothing was wrong. However, remember that we stopped praying, and there was the fact that I was disobedient to begin with. The X-rays showed a small hairline crack left. They placed his foot in a cast, and back home we went. I was in awe of what God had done and frustrated with myself for having been surprised and stopping my prayers. Disobedience is costly! This event opened a door the size of a semitruck for the enemy, and it would create a downward spiral in me that would last until 2012, and change my world forever.

Two Decades, One Problem

This healing shows God's gracious hand to uphold us while we search or even while we don't. Later, during the same year as the above miracle, I began what would become a battle with atrial fibrillation (A-fib) that would span almost two decades before complete healing and restoration would occur.

At this time in my life, my stress level was off the charts. I was dealing with a terminally ill husband, three boys, working nights in a level-one trauma center, and attending nursing school. Later I found out that the nursing school staff was sure I would not make it through the program and talked of my health and stress regularly! In November 2002, I was sitting in my car waiting to return to class for an exam, when suddenly it felt like an engine turned over inside my chest. I had never felt anything like it before, but I had experienced SVT (supraventricular tachycardia) during my pregnancies, and I remembered the maneuvers they did to slow my heart rate. I tried them all, except dunking my head in cold water, but none of them worked. My heart rate was around 147 bpm, but I walked inside and took my exam (yes, I may have been a slight overachiever). As I sat down, one of my classmates told me I didn't look good. I told her I did not feel good, and she told me to go down to the clinic and talk to one of the instructors. I assured her I would go as soon as I took the test. After the exam, I went downstairs to the lab area where one of our instructors was working, and she said the same thing. I told her what had happened in the car and what maneuvers I had tried. She took my blood pressure and could not get one. She said I needed to go to the hospital, so I asked her to take me. The head instructor said that I needed to go by ambulance, but I begged not to. They gave in, so we headed out. As I began to walk, however, I realized I was not going to make it. I turned around and told them to call an ambulance.

Now comes the funny part of the story. We were in the lobby on the first floor of the building, one block from the local fire department. When the first responders showed up, they could not get my blood pressure either. I was very weak at this point and white as a ghost (so they told me). They sent a handful of calendar-worthy firefighters in to get me. They even sent the hook-and-ladder truck! I said to them, "Really, did you think I was on the roof? How embarrassing." They wanted to convert me in the lobby (to use electric frequency to shock my heart back into rhythm). I said, "No, take me one block to the hospital, please." Emory's ER is where I met a doctor I only wanted to see once; thankfully, the attending doctor came later in his place. I was in the hospital for five days on a drip, and my heart was put back into rhythm. However, it did not remain in sinus rhythm, so I needed to undergo an ablation. I debated this procedure for a long time, mainly because I didn't have time for this as a nursing student, mom, and wife. However, the medical staff convinced me, and I am thankful I had a great attending doctor who had done this for a while and knew exactly what it would take to demonstrate my need. That ablation lasted ten years and would have lasted longer had it not been for the stress, which I thought I was managing but which was catching up with me.

In healthcare, we say, "What you do (or don't do) to your body today will show up in the next ten to fifteen years." That is exactly what happened: all the stress I carried ten years earlier caught up with me, and the A-fib returned in 2012 under entirely new circumstances. I had been gaining weight at a ridiculous rate but could not get anyone to pay attention (more about this in chapter 8). In July of that year, I was at work when I suddenly felt very ill and was sent down to the ER. I was in atrial fibrillation, and when they checked my thyroid (thanks to my boss, who instructed them), it turned out I had hyperthyroidism. I was sent to endocrinology for medication to treat both my thyroid and my heart. Within a year the thyroid disease would be gone, and it was determined to have been caused by stress. I was able to stop taking the thyroid medication. Unfortunately, A-fib was not so easy to get rid of; it runs in both sides of my family, which I was unaware of at the time. In my case, episodes were brought on many times not only by frozen drinks, but also from stress (I was in graduate school this time).

The chain of events with my heart would continue like this on and off for eight more years. Within a two-year period, I was cardioverted six times, and then I had another more in-depth ablation surgery, which held for two more years until the death of my son. Then I had two more cardioversions, long-term medication, biannual cardiologist visits, monitoring, sometimes blood thinners, and multiple hospital admissions. The final cardioversion that occurred in late 2020 would be my last. Due to COVID-19, I had been left in A-fib for more than a week, and I could do nothing. I even began having symptoms of heart failure, and that was one thing I surely wasn't going to take!

I want to point out, in case you missed it, that stress is the number one killer of the body! Studies have shown that almost all disease stems from the body's constant exposure to the "fight or flight" response. That is why many dormant, genetically predisposed diseases will show up during pregnancy, without the patient ever having one sign prior to that event. You cannot remain under constant stress and stay healthy. I believe this is one of the reasons we are seeing such an uptick in chronic illnesses. Stress is linked to poor gut health, which then links to all disease, but I will get off that topic before I get too medical. Just remember the body's ability to heal itself.

In early 2021, I decided I'd had enough of this heart trouble. I wanted to be free of it! So I began to seek the Lord about it. In early June, I had weaned down my medication and then stopped taking it. This was not wisdom or the Lord telling me this, and it could have led to trouble. I noticed my heart skipping beats and that it was becoming more frequent, so I sought the Lord again. He told me that He had not told me to stop my medication, and then He told me to return to it and not to stop until He told me to do so. I began the full dosage again, feeling a little defeated (or corrected), but I obeyed.

The Lord brought to my remembrance the healing of my MDD (major depressive disorder), and with that reminder I was full of faith that He would take care of this also. In August 2021, while attending the North Georgia Revival (I attended regularly), I was standing in the congregation when Bishop Lance Johnson spoke to disease and called out atrial fibrillation. I knew it was my time, and I was healed. God said I could stop the medication now, and so I did. Then one evening in mid-September, the devil tried to bring it back to me while I was on a trip to visit family. I stood on 1 Peter 2:24 (NKJV), "by [His] stripes you were healed." I had been off medication for a month without issue; we were close to my cardiologist office, and though I did love and trust my cardiologist and had driven three hours across state lines to see him previously, I wasn't telling a soul about this episode. I already had this victory, and I wasn't going to relinquish it to the enemy! I simply told it to go, in Jesus' name, and I kept going. By that night, I still was in A-Fib and getting angry about it. I knew I had authority over this body, and it was going to listen! I prayed and told God that I was ready for God to be God in my life. I was not going to the doctor or to the hospital, nor was I taking medication for this issue anymore. It was healed! It was going to go, or I was going to be in heaven; either way, I was okay. The next morning, I continued to just go on with my day, knowing that by His stripes, I am healed. I ignored my heart and how it was trying to make me feel. Then about the middle of the day, I checked my pulse, and we were back in normal sinus rhythm, and I had won!

The Enemy Attempts to Steal My Healing

After this healing, I should have not been surprised at all, and I wasn't overly surprised; instead, I was having a dance party because the devil had lost this fight once and for all. I had tried to stand firm in 2020 before the last cardioversion, but the outcome was not the same. This time, however, I knew so much more about my Father, my Jesus, and my covenant authority. I have been off all medication since that day. The enemy would try one final attempt in December 2021, because I opened the door for him. One afternoon, I was short with my mom and was not honoring her, though I did not realize this until the following week. She has a vast collection of Christmas decorations, and she was talking about putting them out, only she couldn't do any of it herself. I had said, "Mom, we aren't putting out all that stuff; we will choose a few," even though I knew it was her favorite time of year. I wasn't in the mood for Christmas; I had just lost my job, and I didn't feel like doing all of that decorating.

The following Monday, while she and I were at lunch, my heart flipped. That night, after my mom was asleep, I sought the Lord on why my heart went into A-fib, since I was healed. The Lord reminded me of the conversation with my mom about decorations and told me I was not honoring her (which is one of the big Ten). I quickly repented, apologized to my mom the next day, and expected this to revert back immediately. It did not, so of course I was still seeking His answer. He showed me multiple times through the day, by Scripture passages and different speakers, that this was not allowed by Him for teaching reasons, but rather that this was through the devil gaining access by my disobedience. I prayed in the Spirit much during the day, but there was no change. Then I took myself to Tuesday night prayer at church. People came and prayed over me, and there were a few things spoken over me. Pastor Jeff said, "The spirit of fear is being broken off of you, and you are not to worry about your heart. God does not want you worrying about your heart." When we left, I felt refreshed, and all the symptoms from the A-fib that satan was trying to get me to focus on had resided. Though my heart was still out of rhythm, I didn't feel bad like I used to. It was no longer the focus, because Jesus was. The next morning, I sat with God, my heart still beating out of sync. I wasn't seeking for healing, because that was done, and I refused to focus on something already taken care of. Instead, I focused only on Him, His goodness, and how much I love Him.

After a few days, seeing that I was focused on Jesus and not my heart, the enemy tried to attack me through the dream world! You have to protect your dreams. What he sent to me would have been terrifying—in the dream, it was terrifying, and it lined up perfectly with my medical mind. I have never even written it down, though I fully remember it. However, God quickened my spirit and showed me that the devil was trying to get me to speak (and give life) to that dream. I knew immediately that if I spoke it, it would cause great fear within me. I would have to start taking medication again, and I would not be able to stop. (Yes, we can lose our healing if we are not diligent.)

The Lord reminded me to cast down that imagination and keep on moving. The enemy finally left me alone in the area of my thoughts, and on December 15, 2021, while I slept, my heart went into normal sinus rhythm. It had been over two weeks since the start, and I had undergone a day and a half of intense battle, during which I could barely breathe and my medical knowledge had started chiming in. I had to get angry at the situation and the devil, to sit up and declare that the medical knowledge must bow to the knowledge of God and His Word! When I was struggling to hold on, I called on Him, the author and finisher of my faith, to be my strength! I have been free from even the threat of atrial fibrillation for over a year now, and I feel the enemy only moved on because he attempted multiple times and lost. However, he didn't leave me completely alone; just the heart.

God Can Use Whomever We Have Available

In 2005, I met a Jewish man I called Dr. W., a man who himself declared that he wasn't a devout Jew. It did make for good conversations at times, and God would use him to help me survive the next five years. He was there to help guide me through the major depressive disorder (MDD) I was completely unaware of. However, in a forty-five-minute consultation, unrelated to MDD, he could see it clearly, along with the breakdown I was about to have. I believe he was divinely appointed by God and gifted by God to see whatever he saw that day. He had the God-given ability that enabled him to help me. You see, he was not a psychologist for adults or children nor families; he was a neuro and geriatric psychologist. He did not see my age group; he saw older adults with dementia, Alzheimer's, and Parkinson's disease. All Dr. W. was required to do on initial consultation was to clear me for surgery, and if I needed more help, he could recommend someone who treats adults. However, God had other plans—and I love that God will use whomever He chooses and who will allow Him to fulfill His purpose at that moment.

During Christmas of 2007, I ran out to build a snowman, but the snow was powder soft (I was not in Georgia). I went down though seventeen inches of snow and landed hard on my feet, which then caused an immediate muscle spasm in my back. At this point I called the front desk of the resort, explained my injury, and said that I needed help quickly because I did not want to repeat the tree-root injury from 1997. They said I could see the naturopath, and so I gingerly walked across the campus to his office. When I arrived and told him about my back, he recommended acupuncture. I had only seen this done in movies or on TV, so I declined this. He asked me why, so I explained that I was a Christian and couldn't have people burning incense and chanting or praying over me. He tried so hard to keep a straight face, but he smiled and chuckled slightly. He promised not to pray, chant, or burn incense, so I agreed to give it a try. I want to say that now, I would not consider acupuncture with just anyone, because it can open doors to the enemy. However, I did not know that then, and it was my only option at the time. I covered myself in the blood of Jesus and laid on the table, and I was absolutely shocked that when I got up from that table in about forty-five minutes, my back was fine. It was like I had never even injured it! I firmly believe God used that practitioner to heal my back, which shows God's mercy and His ability to use whatever means we have available. I went on to find a Christian who practiced acupuncture later, when I was addressing chronic issues, but during that time I had no faith for God to heal those issues (during my time away with Chris). I will give more details about both of these stories in chapter 8.

The Healing-Obedience Connection

These next healings and lessons have occurred while writing this book, as I have been under constant attack in my body. Some have been little things and some have been big things, but they have been almost constant, and one day the enemy literally kept moving from one body part to another! However, this time it was my respiratory system and the ability to breathe (which I find quite important for life). Each time I would awaken to write or begin to even think about what I was writing, a cough would occur. Of course, before 2020 a cough was just a cough, but now we have every known and unknown virus lurking, so then it becomes a mind game (and having a medical brain doesn't help). I rebuked the enemy, commanded the cough to leave, quoted the Scriptures to my body, but it was actually getting worse. It got to the point that I could not take a deep breath; my lungs and back hurt, and now I had all the signs of pneumonia. This continued for several days, and I was fighting my medical mind like nobody's business. Finally, after many nights without quality sleep, I prayed and asked God what I should do now (of course, this is the first thing I should have done). I heard the Lord tell me to call for the elders and have them anoint me and pray over me according to James 5:14–15. So, I contacted the pastor and let him know what I needed so he could prepare that night for our Tuesday prayer meeting.

I have to tell you that this was a real struggle for me, because I do not allow just anyone to lay hands on me. The women of the church had laid hands on me back in 2021, but then I was desperate about my heart, and I wasn't there yet with this (nor did I want to be). For the last fifteen or so years, I have not asked for prayer from elders or from anyone if I did not personally know they believed like me, so this instruction actually brought some anxiety. Soon I realized there was more to this than just healing my breathing, so I prayed and asked God to reveal the issue and to remove it. He showed me where I needed to forgive and get free of past hurts in the church. Then the Lord said to me, "You are not believing in the elders; you're believing in Me."

Even though I didn't feel like going, I went to the church in obedience, expecting to walk away completely healed of the symptoms and free of the issue causing anxiety. The anxiety tried to return again while I was at the prayer service, but I continued to refocus on God and His words to me (that's why *rhema* is a requirement; had I not heard from Him, I most likely would have left). There were more elders at this service than at any of the previous prayer services, confirming that it was designed by God. The elders anointed me and prayed over me, and I was instantly healed. I could breathe, and I could take a deep breath with no wheezing, no coughing, and no pain. I was not the only one healed; there were others. Some were healed instantly, some improved over days, and some are still in the process of healing. Though I am not surprised when God touches me, I was surprised at the lesson God taught me on this occasion (and it actually still runs through my mind). That night, He showed me how we are all connected in the Body of Christ, and that the obedience of one person can unlock freedom for others. Of course, that means that the reverse is also true (more on this in chapter 7).

After the healing of both my physical and spiritual issues, God used this time to reinforce that there is no formula for healing; we cannot just do what worked before without asking Him each time. We must seek God at the first sign of illness or issue of any kind, listen for the Holy Spirit's instruction, and obey what we hear Him telling us to do. As you can tell, I am still learning when it comes to the truths of God (although I do not think we will ever know all of them in this lifetime), and I will go over some of those lessons in detail in the next two chapters.

Lessons Just Keep Coming

A couple weeks after the above healing, another learning opportunity arose while I was preparing for a mini vacation with my husband Todd. Three days prior to leaving, I began having throat and ear pain, along with two days of fever and chills. I was not going to tell a soul; I was not cancelling my vacation, and I knew this was the enemy again. I prayed and asked God, but no definite direction came, so I stood on the Word and thanked God for the blood of Jesus. I took communion daily (which I try to do anyway, but now I made sure not to miss a day). The fever broke, and symptoms subsided except for occasional ear pain. I packed the medicine bag, with my husband's prescriptions for chronic illnesses (his faith in medicine serves as a reminder to me that we each must walk out our own faith in our actions). As I packed the bag, I placed a few extra medications for cold and flu in there, just in case symptoms got worse; after all, I was going on vacation, and I wanted to do some fun things. That decision proved to be a bad choice; no matter how I justified it, I had planned for failure.

That great planned vacation went bad fast, and I ended up unable to do anything I had planned except to rest. God is faithful, merciful, and full of grace, and He teaches us in these moments. He showed me where I went wrong and the place I gave the enemy a door, and then He sent me to urgent care (I didn't want to go, but I went in obedience). I was able to rest, spend time with my husband, and most likely saved some money too. So where did I go wrong? I had used my husband's faith in medicine and my desire for him not to get sick as my excuse to pack cold medicine just in case, because I feared feeling worse (and fear gives the enemy a place). As it turned out, I did not have the flu or COVID-19, but I did have bronchitis, an ear infection, and a valuable lesson in planning, or not planning, to be exact. I would like to say that was the end of the story, but this attack continued for weeks, and the ear pain then switched ears, which is when I caught on that there was more to this than I thought.

When we returned home, I completed the medication prescribed and was not feeling myself. I couldn't think clearly, and I was irritable, tired, and unable to write (which was the enemy's plan all along). It turns out that this was my response to the prescribed steroids, and though I completed them, I decided that I would not be taking those again. During this time when the ear pain was so bad that I could barely swallow, I had continued to stand on the Word, and I expected this to be gone, but it was not. I ended up back at urgent care and self-treating with alternative remedies. I also began asking the Lord again, what is the deal here? Why is this not leaving? Then the Lord showed me where I had entertained gossip (gossip doesn't have to be just bad stuff), which kept that door for the enemy propped open. I repented, and the pain in my right ear was gone the next morning.

I would like to tell you that that was the end of the story, but it was not. Remember I said I went back to urgent care? It was a horrible experience, and I vented about the practitioner to my husband when I got home. I was so angry because I felt they had dismissed me, barely examined me, and had even lost me in their system. That was not the care I would give a patient, so I had not-so-nice things to say about it. Well, according to 2 Corinthians 10:5 that is called having *lofty opinions*, and they open the door to the enemy. The next day, I had ear pain in the left ear, and this time it did not take days to build up to extreme pain; instead, it started there. I was angry now, because I knew that this was all a spiritual attack of the enemy, and I kept unknowingly opening doors. I repented again but the pain did not reside; I woke up the following morning in severe pain and called a friend. We went through all that had occurred, prayed, and sought the Lord for what to do. He outlined the correct regimen for me, and I began it that day. A few days into the natural regimen, I was feeling better, but it just wasn't gone.

That Sunday night, watching the North Georgia Revival online, Pastor Matt Scott was talking about witchcraft. It piqued my interest when he said that if there is something lingering in your life that you can't seem to get rid of, then it is most likely linked to witchcraft. I immediately thought of this blasted ear and throat issue that had been going on for over three weeks! I sat right up and really paid attention as he went through a list of things, many of which I did not realize witchcraft could be tied to (because it provides an open door for the enemy), and he mentioned makeup. I felt the Holy Spirit tell me to check my makeup that I bought just weeks before I got sick. You mean my new, clean, vegan, natural makeup? The feeling would not subside, so I began to search the company. It was not easy to locate the information about the company, but I did find it and there were no real red flags, so I continued to look, because it just didn't sit right. Then I found a video the owner had made, and there it was—the name of the company (which had been abbreviated), along with the connection to Greek goddesses she claimed as well as the crystals she used for well-being. She claims that since they have such great properties, the company crushes them and puts them in our makeup! What?! You mean I have been wearing crystals without knowing it? (Those "healing" crystals have their origins in the demonic realm.) I gathered them all up, including one palette I hadn't even used yet, and threw them in the outside trash, along with the new nail polish I bought that was created under the spirit of rebellion (later I found clear satanic worship on their website). Now before you throw down the book, here was the result of my "cleaning house": the next morning, all symptoms were gone, and I have been fine ever since.

Passing It On

I hope you learned many things from this chapter, with the main one being that Jesus is the Healer of all. It is the enemy who is behind illness, and he is always trying to snare us. I want to share an excerpt with you from Dr. Roberts Liardon's book *God's Generals: Why They Succeeded and Why Some Failed*. The opening story of General John Alexander Dowie tells how he followed an interesting path to learning the truth behind illness amidst a plague that had taken much of his congregation. Dr. Liardon shared an excerpt of Dowie's own writings, and it refers to my favorite verse in the Bible. During a time of unbelievable loss, Dowie writes about the answer he received in prayer:

> Then the words of the Holy Ghost inspired in Acts 10:38, stood before me all radiant with light, revealing satan as the Defiler, and Christ as the Healer. . . . 'Tis satan still defiles, and Jesus still delivers, for He is just the same today.[16]

We need to know the Word in order to fight, how to seek God for revelation, and how to close any doors we have opened unknowingly. I hope you learn from my mistakes: while it doesn't take obvious sin to open doors to the enemy, disobedience will give him a semitruck-size entrance. Remember that healing of the same symptom in the same person can occur differently at different times. Because of this, we need to ask the Lord what He would have us do. After all, He is the creator of these "earth suits" (I have no idea who said it, but it is my favorite description of the body). He had already provided the healing, and He knows what it will take to manifest it.

---

[16] John Alexander Dowie, quoted in Roberts Liardon, ed., *God's Generals: Why They Succeeded and Why Some Failed*, 25.

CHAPTER 6

What the Bible Doesn't Say

WE HAVE ALL heard statements made by those who believe they are helping, who believe they are full of faith, or who don't know what to say. These statements include, "God is teaching you a lesson," "What a blessing it is for God to receive glory in your illness," "God will heal you in His timing," or "If He doesn't heal you here, He will heal you in heaven." I hope I have already laid a foundation for the two that make me just about come out of my skin: "It must not be God's will to heal you," or "Jesus didn't heal everybody." This chapter is all about debunking those wrong things we have learned or heard repeatedly, which got into our hearts and are impeding the promises of God.

Every one of us, from the most renowned evangelist to the girl in the front row of the local church, have some areas in the Word that we struggle with. Unless we are walking around as Jesus and the apostles did, as we were commanded, then we have unbelief or wrong belief somewhere and may not even realize it. While I could easily believe for salvation (or what I thought was salvation), healing was more difficult to understand because of all the wrong teachings out there. I had missed so much, and I had never read through the New Testament from start to finish (I was an Old Testament girl). However, I did know, deep down inside, that what I was being taught or that I saw in church was not the God of the

Bible, not even the God that I knew and read about throughout the Old Testament. I had no idea what to do with those thoughts, if I should go against the grain, or even how to do it God's way.

It wasn't until I found the Generals of the faith that I began to see the God of the Bible show up again *after* Acts and the Epistles. I had questions: "What did the Generals have that we don't? Were they just more special, chosen, like the Apostles?" No, they were only human too. What they believed and preached sometimes seemed harsh, but it made me think and search. They did not make excuses about why healing wasn't at work any longer, or that God may not want me well; for them, there were no grey areas in healing. Although they walked in the supernatural manifestations of the Holy Spirit, some of them still missed it or had wrong beliefs in other areas. I don't go around looking for flaws in ministers, nor do I rejoice when I see them, but their transparent humanity actually gave me hope. They didn't always have it all together or all figured out, yet God still used them mightily, even if some developed or followed wrong beliefs.

Misunderstanding the Word remains a tactic of the enemy, and he can use it on anyone, which is why complete and repeated submission to the Holy Spirit is absolutely essential. Our beliefs should be shaped through study of the Word and, most importantly, through revelation from the Holy Spirit. That same Spirit resides in us, so why not ask Him? The Holy Spirit was there before creation, and He inspired the men who wrote the Bible. We miss His guidance when we base our beliefs on someone else's Bible commentary or on what a minister tells us, without seeking God on it. Seeking God on a message includes taking it to the Word and studying it out for ourselves. I firmly believe that is why at the age of 25 the Lord put a desire inside me to pray, "I know what my pastor believes, and I know what my mom believes, but I need to know what I believe." Ever since that day, that has been my prayer when receiving messages or teachings, and I do this even if the teaching seems right to me.

I have leaders in my life whom I admire and whom I learn from regularly, but I know that not all of doctrinal our beliefs are the same, and that is okay. The beliefs I am speaking of are what some consider non-essentials (not essential to salvation). Although as I write this word, I am convicted by the Lord for calling anything in His Word non-essential! God did not put anything in the Bible by accident, and His words are Spirit and Life. However, the beliefs I am speaking of are those concerning healing, prosperity, and the spiritual gifts as described in 1 Corinthians 12–14. We are all saved, serving the same God, filled with the same Spirit, and headed the same direction; we are just on different walks or at different places in our walk with the Lord (the key here is that we are all walking with the Lord).

Created to Be Connected

We are the Body of Christ, and we are not to be disjointed or separated; instead, we are to be united. What one body part does affects all the others, whether we realize it or not. Our obedience or disobedience affects others, not just our family line, but the others in the Body of Christ. (This revelation only came to me recently.)

My son's death affected the hopes and beliefs of other saints who were looking at our situation and how we believed. The loss of a battle, especially one that ends in death, creates more questions, misunderstandings in the Body of Christ, and unbelief that can cause others to lose their battles or even to give up fighting them. Then the enemy can use this as ammunition against us if we aren't united in one Spirit and grounded in the Word. It is time to tear down denominational barriers, to take the Word at face value, and to love one another regardless of differences. I have been a part of four denominations, and not one of them has all the answers. Instead, they actually need one another in order to create wholeness.

Thankfully, in spite of our inadequacies as the Body, God is still teaching us His truths.

From the teachings between the four denominations, I had areas I struggled with, and I wasn't sure which way to believe. I would read the Word and ask the Lord how or why on various questions, and He would answer. This book came out of those areas and conversations in which the Holy Spirit broke down my denominational barriers. He continues today, teaching me, speaking to me, and revealing truths of Himself in the wee hours of the morning.

One day, the Lord told me to read the Word and just take it at face value. Once I believed that, then I could begin interpreting it or listening to other ministry's interpretations. That is when I found out that the face value of the King James translation was so far from the original Aramaic, Hebrew, and Greek. In fact, we had lost a lot of the original meaning through translations. This text was not only going to be read, but it was also going to be studied, with words looked up and old definitions researched. This brings up another issue: today's dictionaries are changing word definitions to fit society, so those words are also lost in translation. All the more reason we cannot make it, understand it, or know God's truth without the Holy Spirit!

God Is Going to Get You versus God Loves You

Let's tackle the first common erroneous belief, one that I had from early childhood until recent years. This is the belief that God is a dictator sitting in heaven and waiting for us to mess up so He can teach us a lesson. This lie from the enemy arose from a lie my mother was taught, "God is gonna get you!" She passed on this message to me, as she would say this whenever I would do wrong, and that was more often than it should have been. I had this belief so deeply ingrained in me that one day in high school, a few friends and I skipped Spanish class and went into the attic of the English building. While there, I was raped by a boy who I thought was my friend.

I did not tell a soul, because in my mind it was God's punishment for skipping class! Can you see how messed up that thinking is? For those wondering why I didn't scream, the reason was twofold: if we were found, we would get caught skipping class; also, my trust of adults was very low because I had been molested, and because the enemy had desensitized me over the previous seven years through sexual abuse by multiple men and boys. The enemy loves to keep us captive by the lie that God is punishing us; it keeps us quiet, questioning, and even angry with God.

Later, many years later, I found the God of Psalm 23; 103; and 107 (He was always there, I just had no idea who He was). I had quoted and sung Psalm 23 since I was a child, but part of me still had a fear of the other shoe dropping. However, I was discovering that God was actually full of love, mercy, and grace toward us, so much so He would give up everything to save us and bring us back to Himself. Even though the children of Israel disobeyed, which left them wandering in the desert, He still wanted to be with them, and He traveled with them day and night! He doesn't leave us when we are disobedient; He is the God who will never leave us nor forsake us!

The day this lie was completely debunked in my life (it had been partially dethroned, but I still had hints of it) was October 8, 2020. While in a class during Kineo I, the first year of Kineo Ministry Training Center, where I was studying for a diploma in biblical theology, Pastor Karen was teaching us how Jesus' decision to come to earth to redeem us happened even before the fall of humanity. The next morning, as I sat with the Lord, all of a sudden I realized what that meant and what He had done for me. It meant that God chose to lay aside His Divine Nature (He is infinite, omnipresent, and omniscient) to wrap Himself in human nature (flesh and blood confined by time and space) in order to buy us back from the enemy! Even before the cross, He sacrificed for us. He made the big gesture, and oh, how I had misjudged Him! Think about it: He was Spirit (a non-human form); He was God before time began. Remember those thoughts you had as a child of where God was before, how, who—He is that God. Jesus knew before He left heaven and became human that He could never return to that Spirit form, and now He sits at the right hand of the Father, in glorified human form, for eternity! He came down here, He limited Himself to human form, and then He chose (every day He chose His humanity, even though He was God the Son) not to use His Godhood even when they mocked Him, spat on Him, beat Him, and crucified Him. They didn't even kill Him; He gave up His Spirit! He did it all as a human, empowered by the Holy Spirit, so we could follow Him back to the Father. There is so much more to the story than we ever knew (much more than I am telling here). He is unconditional love, and my heart was melted like wax. I pray you can see that there has been no greater love nor will there ever be. He loves you, right where you are, in all the mess, and wrong decisions. *He loves you!*

God Gives Sickness for Lessons

I have searched all through the Bible and cannot locate one place where God the Father or Jesus said, "I gave you this sickness to teach you ________" (fill in the blank). Not once did He say He was using sickness to build character, give patience, or even give sickness at all! If God gave us illnesses to teach us something, then it would be wrong to seek treatment or pray for the Lord to remove it until we had learned our lesson. If God gave me something to teach me, or build character, and I seek to have it removed, then I am in sin because I am refusing to accept God's guidance. That would mean that every person under medical care who believed this lie would be outside the will of God for their lives. Also, if God the Father was using sickness as a teaching tool, then Jesus would have needed to make every one of His disciples' sick, especially Peter (who could have used good dose of patience and humility). Jesus didn't go around making people sick; instead He went around healing all who were oppressed by the enemy!

Another area in Scripture that has been used to support this theory is 1 Peter 5:10, "After you have suffered for a little while, the God of all grace, who called you to His eternal glory in Christ, will Himself perfect, confirm, strengthen and establish you." Here we must reference Strong's and define *suffered*, G-3958: this word refers to the sufferings of Christ or to the suffering of the followers of Christ. Last I checked, Christ was never ill, though He did suffer at the hands of men. The suffering referred to here, and in so many other places in the New Testament, talks of suffering and persecution. *Tribulation* denotes troubles and distresses that result from persecution. By definition, *persecution* is the affliction of pain, torment, or death to others unjustly, most often used to cause someone to renounce their religious principles or beliefs. That being said, Jesus was persecuted; His followers were persecuted; many Christians in various nations today are persecuted. That is not the same as sickness and disease being used to teach a lesson. If Jesus paid the price to remove sickness, then God is not going to use it, because it's part of the curse, not the blessing.

God does say that He will work out everything for our good, and somehow we equate this to mean that He causes things so He can work them out for our good. Can you see how humanistic that sounds? God doesn't need to create any issues; we already have all the ones He needs for building character! Even Adam and Eve were able to mess up a perfect world! Think about children: would you run over them with your car to teach them the lesson of not running in the parking lot or road? Would you break their legs to teach them to sit still? Would you make them blind to teach them to listen better? Can you see that this is as twisted as me thinking I deserved to be raped as punishment for skipping class?

Scripture says in Matthew 7:11, "If you then, being evil, know how to give good gifts to your children, how much more will your

Father who is in heaven give what is good to those who ask Him!" God is a good God, but we have allowed the enemy to cause us to blame Him for the enemy's work. The belief that God uses sickness to teach us lessons is one of the most widespread lies that was ever created, and he used the church to spread it.

God Knows Best So I Accept It

Maybe you believe that God, in His sovereignty, is in control of everything and that He already has everything planned out for us, even concerning who is saved and who is not. God is sovereign for sure, but if we look at Genesis 1:26–28 and 2:19, we see that He chose to give us dominion and authority on the earth:

> 26 Then God said, "Let Us make man in Our image,
> according to Our likeness; and let them rule over the fish
> of the sea and over the birds of the sky and over the cat-
> tle and over all the earth, and over every creeping thing
> that creeps on the earth." 27 God created man in His own
> image, in the image of God He created him; male and fe-
> male He created them. 28 God blessed them; and God said
> to them, "Be fruitful and multiply, and fill the earth, and
> subdue it; and rule over the fish of the sea and over the
> birds of the sky and over every living thing that moves on
> the earth." . . .
>
> 19 Out of the ground the Lord God formed every beast of the field and every bird of the sky, and brought them to the man to see what he would call them; and whatever the man called a living creature, that was its name.

We see that God gave Adam the rule and authority over all the earth, and He even brought the animals to Adam for him to name. Then Adam gave that authority to satan when he sinned, but Jesus bought it back with His blood and returned the authority to us so we could once again see God's will done on the earth. Believing that God has already chosen who receives salvation, healing, prosperity, and who doesn't, is just lazy Christianity.

Look at 2 Peter 3:9, where Peter tells us that the Lord is not willing that any should perish but that all should come to repentance. Using the sovereignty theory, if He does not wish any to perish, then He would sovereignly save everyone, but because He gave us the right to choose, many will be lost. The sovereignty theory would also mean that God allows evil things to happen to children. Can you imagine giving your child to evil, to be taken away by someone you know only wants to harm them? No! And we don't even know how to love the way He does! God's sovereignty is not to be used to excuse us from our responsibility, just as God's grace is not to be used as an excuse to sin.

God's Getting Glory in It

Have you heard others say, "God is getting the glory in your sickness?" The theory of God getting the glory in sickness attempts to use Paul's thorn in the flesh, found in 2 Corinthians 12:7–10, for scriptural support. However, before I dive into the study of Paul's thorn, I want to first recall all the scriptural evidence from chapter 2, "God's Will to Heal: Old Testament Evidence." Then let's think about Jesus, who, according to Isaiah 53:4–5, bore our griefs, carried our pain and sorrow, was wounded and chastised for us, and by whose stripes we are healed. Jesus went about doing what He saw the Father doing, and He repeatedly healed all, according to the Scripture passages discussed in chapter 3, "Jesus and His Healing Ministry." After looking at all those Scripture passages on healing, ask yourself why God would give sickness to anyone when His only Son died to free us from it? Wouldn't that mean Jesus' death and suffering was in vain? I just cannot make that work. Paul journeyed over ten thousand miles by foot through Israel, Syria, Turkey, Greece, and Italy. A physical ailment would have made these distances unimaginable, maybe even impossible (in the natural flesh). The great healing evangelist F. F. Bosworth, in his book *Christ the Healer*, talks about Paul's thorn not being a physical ailment or sickness. He supports this with Old Testament Scripture passages that talked of "thorns" of Israel mentioned in the book of Joshua and in Psalms. He goes on to say that "thorns" in the Bible are always personalities. Paul's "thorn" was demonic, and he even told us where it came from: "a messenger of satan" (see 2 Corinthians 12:7). The King James Version uses the word *buffet*; in *Webster's 1828 Dictionary*, *buffet* is defined as "A blow with the fist; a box on the ear or face; to slap. . . . To beat in contention; to contend against."[17] This would point us to Paul's persecutions as his thorn in the flesh. According to Strong's, this thorn, G-4647, is a divinely permitted satanic antagonism, a current action, and constantly repeated attacks.

I believe it was more than persecutions, because a thorn doesn't come and go; it remains. This implies it was always with him, and Paul wasn't constantly persecuted. Paul mentions "a messenger of satan to torment me." While the Bible doesn't tell us what or who the messenger of satan was, we can take a look at the Scriptures to show us what it was not. Let's consider all the torture Paul physically went through and didn't complain about; if it had been a bodily, physical torment, why would he complain now? Think about how memories could be used by the enemy, and how the Lord would not desire to remove the memories of the very events that brought Paul to Him. This brings us to mental torment, which seems more like a messenger of satan and is more in line with Paul's past.

According to Philippians 3, Paul was from the tribe of Benjamin, a Hebrew among Hebrews, and a Pharisee. He easily could

[17] Noah Webster, *Webster's 1828 Dictionary* (San Francisco, CA: Foundation for American Christian Education), retrieved from https://webstersdictionary1828.com/Dictionary/all.

have been prideful. He knew all the laws, he would have been boastful, he would have prided himself in his knowledge like the other Pharisees, and both God and the enemy knew this. I considered what thoughts might try to return to Paul with a little help from the enemy. I thought how possibly he could still see the faces of those he authorized killing, those men of God, maybe even the face of Jesus as He was being crucified. Although he was a new creature, those memories, those moments, and those faces wouldn't just miraculously go away. Only through Jesus was Paul without condemnation (as we all are). Only through His grace could Paul let those faces and memories go. Only through Jesus could he fight the enemy on this level, "how to, having done all to stand; stand, therefore." I believe this very messenger of satan is how he learned to "cast down imaginations" and "take every thought captive" (see Ephesians 6:13–14; 2 Corinthians 10:5). He went on to write two-thirds of the New Testament, and his writings teach us how to overcome circumstances and believe God above everything else.

We can see from discussing Paul's thorn how many interpretations can come from different translations. It is important that we study the Word comparing multiple translations to obtain a clearer picture and why we must ask the Holy Spirit to teach us as we study. I want to point out that while we tend to think one-dimensionally, the Bible is alive and has multiple dimensions, and it could be that Paul's thorn had multiple levels. However, it could not be an infirmity, sickness, or disease, because that would make other Scripture passages untrue. That would be impossible, since God cannot lie. God could not refuse to remove infirmities, because Jesus already paid for them. According to 1 Peter 2:24, we are already healed. Again, let's err on the side of Jesus!

In God's Timing

The next theory is the theory of God's timing, in which people tell you, "God will heal you in His timing." This one goes with the "delay is not denial" way of thinking about healing. A delay in the manifestation of an answer to prayer is not a denial, and that works for some things, but not for needs that He has already supplied. According to 1 Peter 2:24, healing is already done. That Scripture verse says that we were healed, past tense; therefore, in God's timing, it has already occurred. Healing is also a part of salvation; the word *saved*, given in Romans 10:9–10, is *sozo*, G-4982, and it means "to deliver, protect, make whole, heal." If healing was already provided as part of our salvation, then why would He tell us to wait? Does God tell us to wait to be saved when we ask? No, because then if we died before salvation, we would be eternally separated from Him! Salvation was the entire reason Jesus came. Look once more at 2 Peter 3:9 (NKJV): He is "not willing that any should perish but that all should come to repentance." Therefore, since there is no delaying salvation, and healing is part of salvation, there is no delay in healing on God's part (we will talk about our responsibility in the next chapter).

Next, let's look at timing in Jesus' ministry. Many times, the Bible tells us that Jesus was moved with compassion. He even healed the ear of the man sent to arrest Him—someone who was not even in covenant with Him but was actually against Him. In Matthew 15 and Mark 7, when speaking to the Canaanite woman, Jesus said that He was sent only to the lost sheep of Israel. It wasn't time for Him to be revealed to the Gentiles, and yet here she was: a Gentile asking Jesus for help. Even though it wasn't His time, her faith moved Him, and He healed her daughter. If you still believe it isn't God's time to heal you (though I hope you don't), great faith can overcome that obstacle. Use the Scripture passages in Appendix A to increase your faith.

One Last Time

I do not think I need to return to the most used lie of all, "It's not God's will to heal you," as we laid an entire chapter of groundwork on debunking this one. Remember that Jesus went about doing what He saw the Father doing, so if Jesus was healing, the Father was too! If you need further information in this area, Pastor Derrick Snodgrass taught an amazing series, titled *10 Things Jesus Never Said about Healing*, that you'll want to watch. While I watched I was screaming at my TV like I was at a college football game—I had found someone else who believed just like me, and he was still alive!

Another area that I feel we exhausted already is that "Jesus doesn't heal everyone." This theory just isn't biblical, because the Bible repeatedly tells us that Jesus healed all. The bottom line is that our issues surrounding sickness and disease aren't God's doing. He hasn't caused it, He isn't delaying healing it, and He isn't trying to teach you anything with it. Those are all lies of the enemy. He wants us to blame God so we don't ask Him for help. We get angry, and it causes us to turn away from Him. Jesus went to the cross and gave His life to bring us life. In Strong's, the Greek word *zoe*, G-2222, means life in the absolute sense. It is life as God has it, which the Father has in Himself, and which He gave to the incarnate Son to have in Himself. It is life that the Son manifested in the world. If God isn't sick, and the Son isn't sick, and we have the same life, we aren't meant to be sick either!

> God was always the healer. He is the healer still, and will ever remain the Healer. Healing is for YOU. Jesus healed, "all that came to Him." He never turned any one away. He never said, "It is not God's will to heal you," or that it was better for the individual to remain sick, or that they were being perfected in character through the sickness. He healed them all, thereby demonstrating forever God's unchangeable will concerning sickness.[18]

[18] John G. Lake, quoted in Roberts Liardon, ed., *The Collected Works of John G. Lake*, 508.

CHAPTER 7

Our Role in Healing

FOR THIS CHAPTER you will need to buckle your seat belt, put on your big-girl panties, or as the Bible tells us, gird up your loins, because this flight has turbulence. I have shared with you how God wants us well, how Jesus already paid for our healing, and how Scripture declares it is already done. Then why are most Christians walking around sick? This is the chapter that will shine light in the darkness as you walk with me through some intimate conversations with God, myself, and others. I pray the Lord lands this right in your heart so that you, too, can overcome the enemy and his lies and walk in the divine health the Lord paid for with His blood.

"See, you have been made well, Sin no more, lest a worse thing come upon you" (John 5:14b NKJV). Jesus said this to the man He healed at the pool of Bethesda. We get offended when someone tells us we are in sin, if we read about someone saying sin is the issue, or even now when we hear Jesus saying sin could bring worse things. In December 2022, God showed me that I, too, had a wrong idea of sin and that my definition of sin was the issue. We think of sin as breaking the big Ten, the Ten Commandments, but sin is so much more than this. Here is sin as defined in Strong's in both the Hebrew and the Greek:

> H-2398 (verb): To miss, forfeit, lack; missing the road or

mark. An act of deviating from God's direction. It is an act of sin against God, the Lord, a result of wrongdoing or a perversion of justice.

H-2399 (noun): A crime, or its penalty; sin in the sense of missing the mark; guilt of such an act.

H-2403 (noun): A sin against God; a deviation from a right lifestyle; an act of deviating from that which God has marked out.

G-264 (verb): To miss the mark, not the committal act, but the continuous practice.

G-265 (noun): An act of disobedience against the divine law.

G-266 (noun): The nature of sin, a moral deviation from the principle, a source of sinful action.

The majority of the definitions include "to miss the mark," and we miss it because we don't know the Word, which tells us where the mark is. Therefore, most sin in a believer's life is simply deviating from the plans of God. We do not know His plans or walk in His ways without knowing His Word and His Spirit! John 4:24 tells us that true worshipers, whom God is looking for, must worship Him in both spirit and truth.

In Galatians 5, Paul talks about crucifying the flesh. In this passage, we are repeatedly told to walk in the Spirit, because Paul knows that if we cannot hear from God, then we will not obey God. When we are in the flesh, we don't have the hearing ears or seeing eyes that Jesus often spoke of. Anytime we walk in the flesh, we are walking by the sin nature and not by the Spirit. According to

Galatians 3:10, if we are walking under the law, then we are back under the curse, because to avoid the curse we must keep the whole law, and only Jesus was able to accomplish that. However, the Bible tells us that when we are walking in Spirit, we are free from the law of sin and death, according to Romans 8:2.

The Lord was talking to me one morning as I was starting to awaken. He showed me a family in a home and a thief in the other room. They seemed to know he was there, but they were not doing anything about it. Then the Holy Spirit asked me, "Would you allow a thief to remain in your home if you knew he was there?" I said, "Of course not" (but in fact, that is what I was doing).

The Lord then equated this picture to us, His children, putting up with sickness, pain, and disease. By not taking the authority God has given us over sickness and disease through the stripes and blood of Jesus, that is like finding the thief and telling him he can remain and live there as long as he stays only in that area. But that is not what a thief does! A thief will not obey the laws and will not follow rules you set. He must be removed, and with force when needed. We have the authority to use God's power within us over the thief.

I had this problem with my right knee going on intermittently for a while; I would take authority over it, and it would leave for a time, but when it returned, I was not quick to take authority again. It was not until I had gotten angry or fed up with it that I demanded it to go, which it usually did. But God was saying to me that the moment the pain comes, the moment the sickness comes, the moment you realize disease does not belong to you, that is the moment you should be evicting the thief! Don't allow him to remain in your house, casing the joint and expanding his territory! The longer he remains, the more ammunition he obtains! Jesus paid in full the price for healing all sickness, pain, disease, and injuries. Healing belongs to us, His children, and by allowing the enemy to encroach on our homes (our bodies), we are allowing the thief to live in the house!

> For though we walk in the flesh, we do not war according to the flesh, for the weapons of our warfare are not of the flesh, but divinely powerful for the destruction of fortresses. We are destroying speculations [casting down imaginations] and every lofty thing raised up against the knowledge of God, and we are taking every thought captive to the obedience of Christ, and we are ready to punish all disobedience, whenever your obedience is complete. (2 Corinthians 10:3–6)

The biggest factor in this battle isn't the enemy; it is our lack of knowledge, our unbelief, and the fight happening right between our ears. Below is a quote from the mother of John Wesley, which to me sums up sin perfectly.

> Whatever weakens your reason, impairs the tenderness of your conscience, obscures your sense of God, takes off your relish for spiritual things, whatever increases the authority of the body over the mind, that thing is sin to you, however innocent it may seem in itself.[19]

Why Are So Many Still Sick?

We may not be in sin, but are our souls prospering? We have the responsibility to create the atmosphere for our souls to prosper so that we might be in health. "Beloved, I pray that you may prosper in all things and be in health, just as your soul prospers" (3 John 2 NKJV).

As I was sitting in church one evening, watching many people come for prayer but leaving the same way (or so it appeared), I asked the Lord about it. Before I share with you the Lord's answer, I want

[19] Susanna Wesley, letter to John Wesley, June 8, 1725.

to say that yes, the Lord can be working on the inside of someone before He works on their outside (though Jesus did both, instantly, many times). The Lord responded, "I desire to touch many more people than you see, to heal many more. But while waiting, instead of seeking Me, they are speaking all the lies they have believed. And when they leave, doubt, fear, and the speaking of lies continue so what I desire to do is negated before they even leave the parking lot." I pondered on that, and realized that even when we come for prayer, we speak what we have heard from the doctor as if it were truth. Then we play those words over and over in our heads, and with every replay, we plant another seed of doubt. By the time most people arrive for prayer, they have zero faith and barely any hope, because the enemy has used those words to plant seeds, which starts the lies flowing in their heads.

Our healing is already complete in God's eyes, according to Isaiah 53:3–5 and 1 Peter 2:24, so we are supposed to be defending our healing, not begging for it. We are asking the wrong questions. Instead of asking God for healing, we need to be asking Him for the revelation of healing and what He is saying now to us concerning our issues. Then we must be still, listen, give Him time to answer, and obey when He gives direction.

God speaks to each of us differently, so His tone and way of speaking to me will be totally different that the way He speaks to another person. He knows each of our hearts, and He knows how to speak to them. He will share things with us if we sit with Him and listen, but we have to be ready and prepared for His answer, as God cannot lie or lead us astray. I believe that many times the reason we don't get answers is because we can't handle the deeper truths of the situation. Jesus shows us this to be true in the Gospel of John, when He told His disciples, "I still have many things to say to you, but you cannot bear them now."[20] We believe we are ready for

---

[20] John 16:12 NKJV.

truth, but in all honesty it can be very painful, and there are times we cannot bear it. It can actually do harm if we are not ready or if we don't know the Father's heart, so sometimes God in His mercy remains silent. I have found that after some degree of healing in my heart, and after God sharing His heart, then God will share with me the "why" of a situation. Looking back, I also realize how He tried to help during the situation, but I couldn't see it at the time.

Seeds of Disobedience

This chapter is the most difficult to write, not only because it incorporates the details of the deaths of Mike and Chris, but also because it is about taking responsibility for our role in health, sickness, and disease. It was through this journey, this whole journey, that I have learned just about everything I am sharing with you in this book. I want to start with the elephant in the room: my son's death. I had told you earlier about how God had kept him safe during the pregnancy despite all those attempts of the enemy, so I am sure you're wondering where God was when the enemy succeeded (I know I was). Although I never blamed God for giving Mike or Chris Huntington's disease, I was disappointed in Him for not keeping His word. You will see that this wasn't correct either, but it would be almost four years before God could reveal the truth of what happened. Before I could handle that conversation, I had to learn His heart and His true character, not to mention His Word.

To be totally honest, I wasn't planning on sharing this part, but we all have sinned and fallen short of the glory of God, and that's why we need Jesus! James 5:16 tells us to confess our sins to one another and pray for one another so that we may be healed. With that, let's return to the night of Joshua's broken foot and my act of disobedience that opened the door to the enemy. The night that I brought Joshua home, Mike said to me, "I don't care what you think your God can do; this is my son, and you will take him to the hospital!" Those words pierced my heart and rang through my ears for years. That night, when those words hit my spirit, I knew that short of a miracle, we had just lost Mike's battle. Mike was trying to learn how to believe, but he had watched his mother die of HD, so he knew what was coming, and that left him with no hope inside. I couldn't help him because I was just learning to have faith in God myself, and though we kept praying, trying to expect a miracle, we did not know how to believe and receive, nor did we know anyone who did (we knew people who talked about it, but there was little to no evidence).

In 2005, Mike began to require more attention and care than I could give while raising the boys and working, so he decided that he wanted me to place him in a home. Let me tell you, the day I left him at the VA home, my heart was so broken and hurting. We had tried everything to keep him home, but financially bringing in help was not an option, and insurance didn't cover that for non-elderly individuals. By 2007, I considered myself "single but married," and suddenly I had no idea where I belonged. I still desired to serve the Lord and to remain true to Him and Mike. While my focus remained on the Lord for a time, I was developing a new level of mental health issues when Chris was diagnosed. As time continued, I began drifting further away from God, and the sounds of the world became louder. I heard people say things like, "You deserve to be happy," "You are young, so enjoy life," "Mike would want you to live your life," and "Mike would want you to be happy." In 2009, I had reached what I thought was rock bottom, so I turned to the gym (I needed to change something, anything, or I was going to die). I began losing weight, getting fit, and drawing more attention from men (the latter is dangerous if you don't know your identity in Christ). I started going out with friends a bit more, making more friends outside of church (which isn't always a problem), taking in a little alcohol . . . then a bit more. Next, I was in bars regularly, drinking, singing, dancing, and flirting, all while attending church, first sporadically, and then not at all.

I stopped seeking God completely because I knew I was sinning (yep, the obvious kind) and didn't want to stop; I was having fun and living for me for the first time in my life. After all, I had been raising children and focused on others since I was a child myself, and "I deserved to have some fun" (one of satan's best lies). As a side note, sin is always fun for a time, or else we wouldn't be tempted by it. What I didn't realize is that I was assisting the enemy in building his case so he could devour not only me, but also my offspring. By the time I came to my senses and returned to the Lord, it would be only two more years before the enemy pulled his trump card.

Mike passed away after a fourteen-year battle with this horrible disease, and instead of the disease ending with him, Chris's disease drastically worsened. He went from having a few minor issues to being unable to walk without help, then unable to walk at all. Next he was unable to eat and choking so badly that I had to do the Heimlich while praying for his life. This downward spiral happened so quickly that even I was shocked, and then the thing I swore would never happen, did happen. Chris reached a point that we could no longer care for him at home, because his safety had become a real concern. My heart was even more devastated this time around, and I still had no idea why this had happened, except I knew it wasn't God's will. It would be four years before I could hear God answer that question. As I look back, I can see that through it all God tried to send me help through books and words and by bringing to my remembrance His teachings. However, by this time I was so focused on Chris's illness, graduate school, and my new marriage that I missed God's help. I was already angry, disappointed, and deep in satan's lies, and I didn't know how to get out.

Once I was healed in the waters of the North Georgia Revival, then God could share bits and pieces with me. The more I learned of Him and His heart, the more He revealed. Jesus says many times,

"He who has ears to hear, let him hear!"[21] In His grace and mercy, God continued to try and help me based on the level of faith (or lack of) I was on, until I reached the place where I could hear His truth about the situation and not be destroyed by it. He took me back through my journals, where I saw He had actually warned me of things coming. Since I did not know what He was referring to at the time, I just wrote it down and then forgot about it. He is faithful, and we usually realize it after the battle, but we have to get to the place where we can see His faithfulness through it all!

Know Where You Are

Sometimes we have no idea where we are in a battle, and that is why a close walk with the Holy Spirit is key. God uses whatever He can to get through to us, and He has even used lines in secular movies to get my attention. However, on this occasion, for this teachable moment, He used my work. The previous day in the ICU, we received a patient with sepsis. We noticed the symptoms, started the appropriate treatments, and expected a good outcome. However, when I arrived the next morning, the patient was on the ventilator, the team was placing lines, and the patient's organs had begun shutting down. A few hours later the patient died, and we needed to know why, because we were doing everything right according to the evidence and our (the team's) knowledge of the patient. However, there were things against us that we were unaware of. What we didn't know was the patient had been treated for a previous infection that wasn't fully eradicated, and there had been no follow-up. We thought we had caught sepsis in its early stages, but we were actually at the end stages.

As I drove home that day, very upset at the loss and at the broken healthcare system that claimed another life, the Lord and

---

[21] For example, Matthew 11:15 NKJV.

I began to talk. He said, "You can do everything right and still lose if you don't know what inning you're in." For this patient, we were not in the top of the first, or even in the second or third inning, as we thought; instead, we were in the bottom of the ninth. God wasn't only talking about this patient; this hit my spirit concerning Chris. I felt I had done everything right (healing is a gift that doesn't need earning), and yet I was about to lose. I sobbed all the way home. While God's forgiveness through Jesus' blood does cover our sin, and God never stops loving us, He does not always remove us from the consequences. The consequences affect not only us but also those around us, those we love (and even those we don't). God shows us this through the story of David and Bathsheba: not only did they lose their child (created in sin), but also, from that day forward, the sword never left David's house. In David's lineage (his house) there would be calamity, but out of David's house would come the lineage of Jesus. This shows us how God redeems our mess and turns bad things for our good, even when He doesn't remove the consequences. Still, at this point I had no idea all these things were consequences; remember that John 16:12 tells us that He can't share with us what we cannot bear, and short of a miracle, my son was already gone.

Whose Report Are You Going to Believe?

It was four years after Chris died that I sought the Lord more about the whole situation. The open door was one thing, but why was he ever diagnosed? After all, the Lord had told us, "This disease will die with Mike, and none of your children will have it." Had I misheard Him? What was I missing? As I sat, He said these words, "Whose report are you going to believe?" I still didn't understand. Then He took me back to the day that we went to the clinic to receive Chris's genetic testing results. It was in that moment that everything in me accepted the diagnosis, even before the physician gave it. I already believed the death sentence satan was speaking over my child, and it happened while I was still in the lobby. In that moment, I had lost the battle for real faith. The walk I thought I had, the one I talked about, wasn't true when the battle was about life and death. Everything after that was going through the motions, the works, but there was no real faith; there was only hope, and very little of it.

As we have seen, great faith is not a requirement, but you do need enough faith to ask God, and I had even lost that. In the absence of your own faith, others' faith can help, but I didn't know anyone (at that time) with that kind of faith either. From the outside looking in, it appeared that I was standing in faith, doing everything right (a works perspective). However, in God's sight (a grace perspective), all I needed was to believe His *rhema* over what appeared, what the physicians spoke, and what my eyes saw. Jesus paid the price for this healing, so in God's eyes, it was already done.

Was I responsible, even though I had no idea? No one I knew was teaching this, and all I knew was that it was God's will to heal but I didn't know how. Romans 14:12 tells us that each one of us will give an account of himself to God. I am going to go out on a limb and say that we cannot use "I haven't read that part" as an excuse. Yes, I was responsible, not only for opening doors to the enemy, but also for not seeking wisdom and understanding. According to Proverbs 4:5–7, seeking wisdom and understanding is my responsibility. Hosea 4:6 tells us that God's people perish for a lack of knowledge. I knew I had missed it, and now I could see all the Lord's attempts to get me refocused so He could teach me; however, Chris was already gone. Now the Lord and I would focus on rebuilding me.

Get Rid of Unbelief

I am sharing this with you because God expects us to believe Him over everything and everyone, and He shows us this throughout the Bible (though I have by no means achieved perfection in this). Hebrews 3:19 says, "So we see that they were not able to enter because of their unbelief." The failure of the children of Israel to believe God's Word to them and His power over their circumstances cost an entire generation the Promised Land. At other times, when they believed, they overcame their enemies (or God overcame them), against all odds and many times without even fighting. Jesus teaches us that we need only believe and not doubt in our hearts (different from our head), and we shall receive. I will not say this is easy (though it is supposed to be); it takes focus, and I know how difficult that can be in a world full of distractions. Doubt and unbelief are not the same; a moment of doubt in our minds isn't the issue. We are to take those thoughts captive and speak the Word to ourselves. It is when we allow those doubts from our minds to go unchecked that they plant seeds into our hearts and cross over into unbelief. We are expected to know His Word, which means we must know His Word!

I didn't know His Word enough to fight, and knowing a few psalms, a proverb, and some New Testament Scripture verses from Sunday's sermon will not cut it in difficult times. The only way to rid ourselves of unbelief, or to prevent it, is to know the Word of God so we can say, as Jesus did, "It is written."[22] John G. Lake said, "Faith is a product of your spirit, not of your intellect. Your intellect does not produce faith. Your knowledge may give you ground for faith, but faith is resident in your spirit."[23]

Now I can look back and see that I did not have faith that God was going to take care of me or my family. I had not worked to build my faith in Him through His Word. I did not believe what He said over what the symptoms, lab reports, or doctors said, and that is unbelief.

I had a "works" perspective, and I felt that I must do *x*, *y*, and *z* to convince Him to change the situation. In reality, the only "work" I need to do is to get to know Him more. At the time, I would have

---

[22] Matthew 4:4, 7, 10.

[23] John G. Lake, quoted in Roberts Liardon, ed., *The Collected Works of John G. Lake*, 595.

fought anyone, including God, if they said that I didn't have faith. God tells us that His Word "is living and powerful, and sharper than any two-edged sword, . . . and is a discerner of thoughts and intents of the heart."[24] The only way to discern our own motives or beliefs is to feed on the Word. We will fail if we attempt to figure it out on our own. We must be honest with ourselves, and then God can show us the areas He needs to work on inside us.

Forgiveness Is Key

Mark 11:25–26 (AMP) says, "Whenever you stand praying, if you have anything against anyone, forgive him [drop the issue, let it go], so that your Father who is in heaven will also forgive you your transgressions and wrongdoings [against Him and others]. [But if you do not forgive, neither will your Father in heaven forgive your transgressions]." Right there in Mark, along with a few other places in the Bible, God tells us that to be forgiven we must forgive. Jesus goes on to say that we must even forgive our enemies. We all know about forgiveness, and I will say that most of us need to do it on one level or another, but how do we forgive those who have harmed us so deeply?

We cannot expect healing in our bodies if we are holding ourselves captive with unforgiveness. I had a myriad of reasons not to forgive the men who abused me, and I felt justified about it, but according to the Bible I had to forgive them. Jesus forgave those who were persecuting Him, and Stephen forgave those stoning him to death, but how? Some things are easier to forgive, but then there are those other things, the horrible things that change our lives, the way we see ourselves, or the way we think. The only way I know how to forgive the people connected to those things is to ask God to help

---

[24] Hebrews 4:12 NKJV.

us change our hearts. Yes, we must make the first move, and then God can take over from there. We even forgive by faith!

One day I was in a support group, sharing that I hated my dad (I was a teenager, and this anger had gone unchecked for years), when a lady came to me and said that the way to overcome that hatred is to forgive him. I knew the Bible said to honor my father and mother, so I agreed to give it a try. She told me that every day when I wake up, I should simply say, "I love my dad," even if I didn't mean it at all. I just needed to say it every day. Then, in the same way, I should say, "I forgive my dad." I felt like this was all pointless, and I did not have any desire to forgive him or love him (however, I want to clarify that my father never touched me inappropriately and was not one of my abusers). After about thirty days of repeating these phrases daily, I wasn't saying these things through clenched teeth. Then, in a few months, I really didn't hate my dad anymore. The real miracle of my heart occurred somewhere around the one-year mark, when not only had I forgiven him, but I also loved him more than I ever thought possible. Somewhere between the clenched teeth and the freedom, God had placed His love for my dad inside me, and it remains there to this day. This love is unconditional, has no strings, no expectations, and it gives without needing return.

I took a different approach for the men who abused me and the boy who raped me (and those who stood around without helping). Those actually weren't as difficult for me as I thought they would be; yes, they hurt my physical body and my mental state, but I had nothing invested in them, so it wasn't as deep of a spiritual pain. Through the years, I have had to forgive them on different levels, but it had been years since I felt any feelings that would require a revisit of forgiveness. Then one morning last year, Jesus highlighted to me His statement from the cross, "Father, forgive them, for they know not what they do." I remembered how seriously God took defilement of our bodies, and I realized that those men had no idea what they were doing. Yes, they knew right from wrong, but had they known how God sees the sins against the body, if they had an eternal perspective, a spiritual perspective, then they would never have touched me. Suddenly, I was in tears, not for me, but for their children and their families, who I hoped had no clue of their past. Through those tears, I was able to release the men, and even pray a blessing over them, their children, and their future family generations. I do not desire that their sins carry over into their children. Though I had forgiven them and I didn't desire evil for them, I would have never thought or desired to bless them. However, that is exactly what the Bible tells us to do!

I have just spent the last three years sitting at the feet of Jesus, learning of Him and His love. I have allowed Him to show me all of my issues so we can remove them together, and I can be free in both spirit and flesh. I am not superhuman, and this is not something that can be done by our will; this is the healing of the soul that only Jesus can bring. I promise that no one is worth missing out on God, and if Jesus can forgive those spitting on Him, pulling out His beard, and nailing Him to a cross, then we can forgive others who trespass against us, even ourselves. To forgive is to be free to give and receive love, and we all need Jesus' love.

We must also forgive ourselves! In Matthew 12:25, Jesus says, "Any kingdom divided against itself is laid waste; and any city or house divided against itself will not stand." We are the "house," the "temple of the Holy Spirit,"[25] and when we are divided against ourselves, we cannot stand! That unforgiveness and those thoughts against your own self, the ones that do not line up with God, are a door the enemy uses to bring sickness and disease. Forgiving oneself is probably one of the most difficult things to do, because first you have to admit the wrong to yourself and get over the disappointment you feel in yourself. Then you have to choose to leave those hurts at the feet of Jesus and not pick them up again. Forgiveness

---

[25] See 1 Corinthians 6:19.

of self can be done the same way I described above in the story of my dad and me; you don't have to mean it when you start. God just needs our words, and He can use those to change our hearts. Wake up each morning and declare that you forgive yourself and that you love yourself. Don't think the enemy won't attempt to bring those old thoughts back, but that is where knowing who we are in Christ comes in and causes us to overcome.

Who Are We Really

Jesus cursed the fig tree because it had no more purpose once it was not bearing fruit. That is no different than me throwing a pen in the trash that doesn't write. Though it may still be filled with ink (and even if it is not), its purpose is to enable me to write. Once it no longer works in that way, it no longer needs to remain; it is trash.

We hold on to things that no longer serve a purpose, dead things, things we should throw out. We cling to things we think on from the past, and we cannot move forward until we let them go. We cannot live in the past; we should only remember those things God brings to our remembrance. Everything else we must leave in the past in order to move forward. Once we are honest with ourselves and God, and we stop dwelling on the past, then He can begin to build us up, and we can learn our identity in Him.

We do not base out identity on our bodies, our jobs, our families, our income level, or the things of this world. We must base who we are on the Word of God, where God Himself tells us who we are. We need to know who we are in order to come boldly before the throne, to ask and know that we have received even before we see it in the natural flesh. I am only going to touch on this subject briefly, because this is a lifelong journey; there are multiple levels, and there have been many good books written about our identity in Christ that can help far more than I can (see Appendix C). Our true identity is all about knowing that we are made in His image; we were given the keys to the kingdom of God through Jesus' death and resurrection, and the Spirit of God, who raised Jesus from the dead, lives inside of us! Now let's break this down a bit further.

Genesis tells us that God made us (male and female) in His own image. Then He blessed them and gave them every provision they required, including love and communication. The Word tells us that in the Garden the Lord God came and walked with them daily. Matthew 6:25–34 tells us how God cares for the birds and the flowers, and how we mean so much more to Him than these. The problem isn't believing what the Word says (though first we must read and study); we want to believe that more than anything. The problem lies in ridding ourselves of the world's perception, the enemy's lies, the chatter in our heads, what people have said, even what we have said or our loved ones have said. We need the eyes to see and ears to hear that Jesus talked about to help us with this.

Jesus came to give us life. The Bible says, "If anyone is in Christ, he is a new creation; old things have passed away; behold, all things have become new."[26] That means all the things you did or who you thought you were gets thrown out when you come to Christ. We should not dwell on it; God doesn't see it, and neither should we. As you daily commit to learning who you are in Christ, I pray for God to give you the eyes to see yourself the way He sees you, both physically and spiritually. Continue with the washing of the Word by reading Scripture passages about your identity in Christ and speaking them over yourself daily. Now that we have forgiven and we are learning who we are in Christ, let's take back the territory that belongs to us!

Not Every Thought Is Yours

I was fifty-one years old and sitting in a classroom, and my teacher,

---

[26] 2 Corinthians 5:17 NKJV.

Dr. Smith, said, "Not every thought you have is your own!" Wait, what?! You mean I am not really the one thinking these things? It's not my own thoughts trying to doubt God? Learning that not all thoughts are mine was a game changer for me. It was the beginning of learning how to take thoughts captive according to the Scriptures.

The enemy attempts to plant thoughts in our heads that are contrary to God's Word, and if we are not careful to recognize them, we accept them as our own. When we accept his bad thoughts or suggestions, then we begin to talk negatively to ourselves. Not only does the enemy want us to tear ourselves down in our thoughts, but he also wants us to speak them. Let's say I wake up one morning feeling particularly aggravated with my body. At that moment, I have a choice: I can either sit and think the negative thoughts the enemy is about to provide me, or I can stop and thank God for being alive and for all the good things about my body. On this particular day, I chose to wallow in my faults or negative body traits and to think about all the parts I want to change. Then, since misery loves company, the enemy chimes in and begins whispering, "You are ugly; you are unwanted; you have failed to lose weight so many times in the past, and this one will be no different." Next, he will begin to attack any unhealed areas of trauma, disappointments, or past failures and start the comparison trap. Because I allow it, he continues, "You're such a failure; look where Jane and Joe are now, but you have wasted your life, and your children hate you." Before we recognize it is him, we have joined in, and now we are thinking how horrible we are, what bad Christians we are for thinking such things, the disciples didn't think such things . . . and it can go on for hours, days, week, months, and even years. He can so quickly drag us down and make us think these are our thoughts, but they are not! So what do we do to stop this downward spiral? We speak God's Word to him, to your mind, and to your emotions, standing in front of the mirror if need be.

This is a must if we desire to walk in healing, because thoughts become words and words have power that will bring what is spoken to life. Remember, God spoke everything into existence! The enemy is going to try anything to get us to speak disease and death. We can lose our healing through the words we speak, which begin as thoughts we allow. We have to stand and declare, according to 2 Timothy 1:7, that we have not been given the spirit of fear but of power, love, and a sound mind. We must pray, as David did, "Set a guard, O LORD, over my mouth; Keep watch over the door of my lips."[27] These two actions are only the beginning.

When thoughts come in that do not match the Word of God, or they are contrary to the promises of God, or they do not align with Philippians 4:4–9, then we must stop, tell them to go in the name of Jesus, and speak the Scripture passages that counteract those thoughts. Let's look at the above scenario. I first need to tell the enemy to shut up, and then I need to tell my mind to line up in Jesus' name. Once I have done those two things, I begin to quote Scripture: Psalm 23; Psalm 103:1–5; Psalm 107; Psalm 118; and Philippians 4:4–9 are just a few. I will also throw on some praise and worship music, and in a short amount of time I will be back up and ready to conquer the world.

The struggle isn't always relieved in minutes, and I may have to do this many times a day, but taking our focus off ourselves and putting it on God will always bring relief. When I was battling major depression, it was a little more difficult, but I had also allowed the enemy to speak to me for years, and I had accepted his thoughts as mine. We can be delivered and set free in a moment, but remaining free is our responsibility, and it can be a process. It is a daily decision to choose God, His words, and His promises over what we feel, think, or see. When we conquer this, the enemy doesn't just go away. Though he may stop trying your thoughts for a while, he returns and hopes you have forgotten how he works or how to fight him.

---

[27] Psalm 141:3 NKJV.

If he cannot win with our thoughts, he comes at our dreams even more, and that is where knowing how to cast down imaginations can save your life.

Casting Down Imaginations

Genesis 11:1–9 is the story of the tower of Babel, and this Scripture passage is often used to show how evil and prideful man was (and is). What I hadn't heard taught was that even God took notice of what these men were doing. The Bible doesn't say He took notice because of their pride or their evil ways. The Bible tells us that the Lord actually said that because they set their minds and actions in one accord, no evil thing they imagine would be impossible for them. Even in doing evil, they had the power to accomplish anything they imagined. The power of the mind was sitting right there in Genesis all along. Even the sinful world uses this principle; they call it the "law of attraction," meaning that whatever you think about or imagine about will eventually come to pass. Entrepreneurs, multimillionaires, and elite athletes testify of how they trained their minds and their thought processes to imagine themselves succeeding long before they succeeded. Our imagination is a gift from God, and it is so strong that the Trinity (the text actually says, "Let Us go down,"[28]) came to earth to investigate and put a stop to men doing what they imagined. Our imaginations must be kept in line with God and His Word. That is why we are to think on things that are true and pure.[29]

Have you ever had a bad dream, and the first thing you do when you wake up is to tell someone about it? That is a trap of the enemy! I never realized how vulnerable we are when we sleep. If we leave our minds unguarded, satan works at planting seeds in our imagination as we sleep! God showed me this truth in August

[28] Genesis 11:7 NKJV.

[29] See Philippians 4:8.

2021. I mentioned a few chapters ago how vivid my imagination is, and this can be great when it is used for God. However, those vivid imaginations can also become very real dreams. I have experienced a few in which I was fighting for my life, and somehow I knew it was more than just a dream. The last occasion this occurred was after my initial healing of A-fib. On this night, since I had just spent time with God, I did not pray about guarding my mind as I slept, nor did I have a song or verse in my heart to sing or say right before falling asleep. This was a practice I started earlier that year that had changed my sleeping and my waking; however, I want to say that we cannot allow fear to drive this. Yes, I want my last thoughts before bed to be of God, but if I fail to do so one night, I cannot fear what might happen. Psalm 121 tells us that He protects us, and He does not sleep. Our faith and trust are in Him, not in the prayer, the song, or anything else we do.

Back to my story; I was asleep and dreaming, and the enemy began to use my medical knowledge against me. He began showing me all the things that can occur as a result of A-fib, and he actually showed me my worst fear (and I don't fear death). When I awoke in my real life, I knew immediately what satan was trying to do. He expected I would wake up and tell this dream and give him a place, because that is what I had done my whole life. I usually like to talk about my dreams with my husband or my friends, and by so doing, I speak them and bring them into the realm where the enemy lurks. The Holy Spirit spoke quickly and firmly and instructed me not to speak the details of the dream to anyone. Suddenly, I knew that had I spoken and went about my day with business as usual, my worst fear would have come upon me, and it all began in the area of my imagination.

While we are speaking of worst fears, let's talk about searching symptoms online. This is a practice we medical professionals call "consulting Dr. Google," and it is a tool of the devil for two reasons. First, because we are searching for the world's answers, not God's, and second, more importantly, because it creates doubt, discouragement, wrong imaginations, and fear in us. When we read about all the diseases that have the same symptoms we are experiencing, then our imaginations go wild! We did this in nursing school a lot; every time we began studying another disease, we would hear someone say, "Well, that explains it; I have those symptoms." Health-care students are the worst about self-diagnosing while studying. It is by God's grace alone that I made it out of nursing school alive, for many reasons. Allowing our imaginations to run with the answers that our search brings, which are most likely wrong, gives the enemy a large playground. Then we think on those things and speak those things, which means he can bring them into our life.

We are responsible for guarding our minds to create the atmosphere for God to plant seeds. We do this by not allowing worldly things to be the last thing our eyes see or that our mind focuses on. Instead, at or before bedtime, we meditate on God's Word, pray, sing a worship song, read a faith-filled book, or listen to some instrumental worship music. Do whatever you need to do to tune your heart to God before you go to sleep. When we have those dreams and imaginations, measure them against the Word of God, and if they didn't come from Him, don't you tell a soul! Don't even speak them to God; do not allow them to be spoken out of your mouth. He already knows it anyway! It is hard not to tell, but we have to learn to be quieter and wiser in choosing what to speak and what not to speak.

Deuteronomy 30:19–20 says, "I call heaven and earth to witness against you today, that I have set before you life and death, the blessing and the curse. So choose life in order that you may live, you and your descendants, by loving the LORD your God, by obeying His voice, and by holding fast to Him; for this is your life and the length of your days, that you may live in the land which the LORD swore to your fathers, to Abraham, Isaac, and Jacob, to give them."

The Power of Words

As children, we used to say, "Sticks and stones may break my bones, but words will never hurt me," but actually, words can kill you!

We have the choice to accept someone else's words or not, but our own words can be deadly. Remember that according to Proverbs 18:21 (AMP), "Death and life are in the power of the tongue, And those who love it and indulge it will eat its fruit and bear the consequences of their words." This is why both God and the enemy wants us to speak: the enemy wants us to speak death, while God invites us to speak life. However, we can only speak life out of a clean heart, and the only way that I know to clean our hearts is to focus on God and allow Him to wash over us as we daily meditate on His Word. Our self-talk should reflect the great love God has for us, enough to send His Son to die for us. Use His words, not past words, hurtful words, or the world's words. Philippians 4:6–9 teaches us how to meditate on the Word and how to think on good things (using His definition of good, not ours). Matthew 12:36 tells us that we will give an account for every idle word spoken! And Matthew 12:37 says, "For by your words you will be justified, and by your words you will be condemned." "Death and life are in the power of the tongue" (Proverbs 18:21). The power of the tongue works in all people of the earth; it is just like the law of gravity, and it is working whether you believe in it or not. We are cursing ourselves without realizing it. Every time we say something about ourselves that does not align with God's Word, we are cursing what God has blessed. Because we are created in God's image, our words have power, so we need to use them for our good, and not against ourselves (the enemy already does that). Instead, we should be saying what God says about us and our situation, even when it sounds to the world like we are in denial of the facts.

Let's look at Elisha and the Shunammite woman in 2 Kings 4. The Bible tells us that after her child of promise had died, she returned to Elisha for help. He asked her, " 'Is it well with you? Is it well with your husband? Is it well with your child?' And she answered, 'It is well.' "[30]

She had the opportunity to tell the facts; she had the opportunity to tell the natural truth that her son, the one Elisha prophesied, was dead, or if she had faith, she could have reported, "He was sleeping," but she did not! She said something that appeared crazy, in total denial.

Now that woman had faith I could not fathom, and I am still working on it. Some days I am closer than others. There is another story of faith that has inspired and baffled me, a more recent person who wrote a song I grew up singing in church. One day, when Pastor Derrick was preaching on the Shunammite woman, I was reminded of that hymn, and I began to weep. God showed me the part of his story I was missing. While in the middle of the ocean, in the place his four daughters had died, Horatio Spafford penned the hymn "It Is Well with My Soul." How could he say, "It is well," when he had just lost his four children? I couldn't say that after only losing one. I just could not understand how he could write such a song in the midst of such tragedy. Then God made me realize that Horatio wasn't feeling "it is well." He was still the grieving father of four children lost; he was still the businessman who had lost most of his investments in the Great Chicago Fire two years earlier. Still, there he was declaring that he knew God was in control! He knew what the Word of God said, and he chose to speak truth that would in turn inspire people for centuries. It wasn't a feeling; it was faith!

What a prophetic moment in the darkest of times! We need to learn from those who spoke from what appeared to be denial but was actually faith! Speaking God's truth over our circumstances, feelings, and facts is the power of the tongue! There is nothing wrong with telling the facts, or the natural truth, but in doing so,

---

[30] 2 Kings 4:26 NKJV.

you won't have the opportunity to walk in God's way. However, when we choose to speak what God says, we stand on our faith, and "without faith it is impossible to please Him [God]."[31] To speak the truth we must know the truth, and I hope by now we have realized the importance of studying God's Word.

Whose Faith Is It?

I was taught that only through your faith can you be healed. I understand where that thought comes from, and it has a level of truth. However, teaching that this is the only way to be healed is more dangerous than teaching that miraculous healings ended with the Acts of the apostles. This teaching leaves people hurt, mad, disappointed in God, and thinking that God did not love them enough. Nevertheless, I knew that it was always God's desire that we be healthy and not sick. Why? Because that was part of His Son Jesus' death and exchange for us through the cross. Faith is a complex subject, but Jesus says in Mark 11:22 (NKJV), "Have faith in God." He doesn't say to have faith in healing or in provision, but to have faith in the One who is the Healer, the Supplier of needs, the Giver of gifts. How can we have faith in someone whom we are afraid of or whom we do not know?

According to Romans 12:3 (KJV), we are all given "the measure of faith." I can give a pencil to an infant, and they will have possession of it, but they will have no idea how to use it. Worse, they can actually hurt themselves attempting to use that which they do not have the knowledge to support. We all possess faith, but our levels vary depending on how we cultivate it, and our cultivation depends on our knowledge of God (not knowledge about God). Our knowledge of God comes from studying His Word and close fellowship with Him. In that way, faith and fellowship are directly correlated. The more fellowship you have with Him, the greater your faith will be.

---

[31] Hebrews 11:6 NKJV.

We tap into this on different levels. Some people have basic faith, some have great faith, some have faith to go to God with prayer and supplication, and some only have enough to go to church when a friend asks. Some have enough faith to believe God is using doctors and medicine to heal and take care of their issue. Others have faith to allow the Great Physician to fix their problem once and for all. There is nothing wrong with any of these levels; according to Scripture, the key is that it all be done in faith. You cannot walk in someone else's faith; you must walk in your own. Romans 14 is an excellent source concerning faith; Paul is writing in the context of food, but the last line in the chapter says, "For whatever is not from faith is sin."[32] That means that everything I do must be done according to my faith. Zechariah 4:10 tells us not to despise small beginnings. Likewise, do not be ashamed of what level of faith you have; only work to increase it. "Faith comes by hearing, and hearing by the word of God."[33] Read the Word out loud so you can hear it, and ask God to help you in understanding. This will also work to increase your fellowship with God. My faith is greater than it used to be, but it is still not where I believe it should be or where God says it should be, according to Scripture. The Scriptures tell us "faith is the substance."[34] Faith is for the now; we cannot have faith for tomorrow or for yesterday. Faith is only today.

As I mentioned above, for many years I saw people who were seeking healing but were hurt or turned away and rebuked for not having the faith to be healed. Then I learned that in most cases, it is not the sick person's faith that is to provide the healing.

> Is anyone among you sick? Let him call for the elders of the church, and let them pray over him, anointing

---

[32] Romans 14:23 NKJV.

[33] Romans 10:17 NKJV.

[34] Hebrews 11:1 NKJV.

> him with oil in the name of the Lord. And the prayer of faith will save the sick, and the Lord will raise him up. And if he has committed sins, he will be forgiven. (James 5:14–15 NKJV)

See in this text where the elders are called for prayer, and the prayer of faith will save the sick? Whose faith is required? The elder's faith! Not the sick person's faith. The only faith the sick person is required to have is the faith to call for the elders. But the false teaching came about when ministers no longer exhibited the power of God in their lives or their ministry, and instead of self-examination, they created this theology to cover their inadequacy. In essence, they were taking the burden of faith off of themselves and placing it on the one who is was already burdened with sickness and disease. Jesus rebuked His disciples when they failed to do as He commanded. Even so, Jesus never rebuked any of the sick people for lacking faith, not even the man at the pool of Bethesda.

In 1 Corinthians 12, Paul mentions the gift of faith. This faith is different and is a manifestation of the Spirit. Smith Wigglesworth talks about how the gift of faith isn't something you walk around with all the time; it comes and goes (he would know; he's called the apostle of faith). It is a gift from God that requires extreme circumstances, like a life-and-death situation. Like Daniel in the lions' den, the three Hebrew boys in the fiery furnace, and John in a pot of boiling oil, to name a few. When you are at a place where you reach the end of your faith, God will give you His! Howard Carter, the founder of England's first Pentecostal Bible School, confirms this in his book *Questions and Answers on Spiritual Gifts*. Mr. Carter mentions that once a person has experienced the gift of faith, it never leaves, and it should be available to them at their time of need. I have not reached this place yet (and I'm not really asking to, since it requires such extreme circumstances), but I have read countless stories about it occurring in people's lives and circumstances, which in turn gives me faith.

Yes, personal faith plays a part in healing, and it plays a part in various ways. The best explanation of this is found in the first volume of Roberts Liardon's *God's Generals*. He writes that at the time of altar call, Smith Wigglesworth would say, "If you move forward only a foot, you will be blessed; if you move forward a yard, you will get more. If you come up to the platform, we will pray for you, and God will meet your needs with His supply."[35]

In the Bible, some people, like the woman with the issue of blood, were healed by their faith, as they reached out and took healing that was available. However, not all who were healed had that kind of faith. Some only had enough faith to come to hear and see; some had faith enough to ask for healing. Some didn't even have that much faith, and Jesus came looking for them. All of those are different levels of faith, yet Jesus healed them all. Only God knows the level of faith that someone is operating in, and He will meet them there in their faith. "Have faith in God"![36]

We should not compare what God does for one with what God does for another. Unless you are comparing yourself to Christ, comparison is a tool of the enemy, and it leads to the loss of our graciousness, our thankfulness, and our joy. It gives the devil a foothold: not only is it coveting (a sin against one of the Ten Commandments), but it also lessens God's ability to move in our lives. I have been guilty of this for sure. I have asked why He raised up or healed this person or that person and not my son. I even struggled with being happy for the victories in healing that other people experienced. But God is God, and He is a good God. Comparing takes our focus off of God and onto lack, and what we feel is missing.

---

[35] Smith Wigglesworth, quoted in Roberts Liardon, ed., *God's Generals: Why They Succeeded and Why Some Failed*, 215. Used by Permission.

[36] Mark 11:22 NKJV.

With our eyes off God, we begin to slide backward and move out of fellowship because we are hurt, we are disappointed, and we think God is unfair. Instead, we should recognize when the new convert received radical deliverance of all addictions, even though you had been asking to be free of cigarettes for years. We should rejoice with them. You should rejoice when sister so-and-so is healed of diabetes, even though you still take insulin. Why does rejoicing with others matter? For one thing, the Bible tells us to, in Romans 12:15; for another, what God does for one, He will do for another. It should bring us hope to know we have evidence of His power, and that we, too, can have our healing manifested! Remember, He is not a respecter of persons. Pray the Word and bring it back to His remembrance, according to Isaiah 43:26 (NKJV), "Put Me in remembrance; Let us contend together; State your case, that you may be acquitted."

Let us have faith in God, use our faith in God to help others, and celebrate one another's victories. We are all one Body in Christ.

Precedence Is the Law of First Mention

In a court of law, *precedence* is a situation where a previous case that was tried previously in court received a verdict that can then be used as a guideline to assist in the current legal case. In chapter 3, we talked about the different ways healing and deliverance took place in the New Testament. These examples written in the Word are what we call *precedence*, or the law of first mention. In my opinion, this is why only certain miracles are listed in the Bible; there would be no need to write so many if they were healed in the same manner, according to this law. With the understanding that God is never changing and is not a respecter of persons, we can use these biblical examples as precedence to stand for healing now. Let's quickly go back over the healings listed in Jesus' ministry (excluding raising the dead).

1. The first leper (Matthew 8:1–4; Mark 1:40–45; Luke 5:12–

15).[37] He asked, "Lord, if You are willing." (No overcoming faith here.) Jesus was moved with compassion and said, "I am willing, be cleansed." And immediately his leprosy was cleansed.

2. The centurion's servant (Matthew 8:5–13; Luke 7:1–10). Yes, this healing was done through faith, but not the servant's faith. The servant was the recipient of the healing.

3. Peter's mother-in-law (Matthew 8:14–15; Mark 1:29–31; Luke 4:38–39). Jesus came into the house and saw His disciple's mother-in-law lying sick with fever, so He touched her hand, and she rose up and began serving. There is no mention of anyone's faith actually being used; Matthew did not even mention the disciples asking Him to heal her. Mark does mention the disciples speaking to Him (verse 30), and Luke does say they "besought Him."[38] Jesus did not command anything from her; He saw a need and met it.

4. The paralytic man with friends (Matthew 9:1–8; Mark 2:1–12; Luke 5:17–26). Jesus saw their faith (the text doesn't say the man's faith, but that of his friends), and He forgave the man's sins. Then afterward He healed him to prove His authority on earth.

5. The woman with issue of blood (Matthew 9:20–22; Mark 5:25–34; Luke 8:43–48). She had faith in who Jesus was. She initiated the contact, broke all the Jewish rules, and was healed.

6. Jairus' daughter raised from dead (Matthew 9:18–19, 23–26; Mark 5:21–24, 35–43; Luke 8:40–42, 49–56). Jairus had faith for Jesus to raise his daughter from the dead. Jesus came and turned out all who were mourning her (He turned out all those who believed only what they saw in the natural; you have to turn out the unbelievers or those who have don't have faith with you). He then took the girl by the hand, and she arose.

7. Two blind men (Matthew 9:27–31). They were yelling for Jesus to have mercy on them. Jesus asked them, "Do you believe that

[37] Scripture quotations for this story are taken from the NKJV.

[38] Luke 4:38 KJV.

I am able to do this?" They said, "Yes, Lord," and He touched their eyes, saying, "It shall be done to you according to your faith."

8. The man with the withered hand (Matthew 12:9–13; Mark 3:1–5; Luke 6:6–10). Jesus was in the synagogue, and there was a man with a withered hand, Jesus healed him to prove to the Pharisees it was lawful to heal on the Sabbath. There is no mention of the man asking, but he did follow through in obedience when Jesus told him to "stretch out your hand," so he had enough faith to obey.

9. The boy with a demon (Matthew 17:14–21; Mark 9:14–29; Luke 9:37–42).[39] The boy's father asked Jesus, "If You can do anything, have compassion on us and help us." He did not even have faith that Jesus could do this. Jesus told him, "If you can believe, all things are possible to him who believes." His son was delivered, but before the spirit left him it distressed him greatly (it put on an ugly show; don't give up when things look worse than before).

10. The deaf-mute man (Mark 7:31–37). He was brought to Jesus, and Jesus took him aside, spit and touched his tongue, and placed His fingers in his ears, but nothing happened. Then looking up to heaven, He sighed and said, "Be opened!"

11. The crippled woman in the synagogue (Luke 13:10–17). Jesus was teaching in the synagogue, and He saw her. Then He called her to Him and said, "Woman, you are freed from your sickness." No faith was required, but she was in the synagogue. She did not ask, but He saw the need.

12. The man with dropsy (what we now call edema) (Luke 14:1–4). Again, Jesus was talking to the Pharisees about healing on the Sabbath. He was in one of their houses eating when He saw the man (so this man would have been associated with the Pharisees and lawyers, not a poor destitute man at all), took him, healed him, and let him go. No faith, no asking; Jesus saw the man and healed him, and then He talked about it.

---

[39] Scripture quotations for this story are taken from the NKJV.

13. The ten lepers (Luke 17:11–19). [40]They yelled for Jesus to have mercy on them, and Jesus commanded them, "Go, show yourselves to the priests." As they went (as they obeyed), they were healed. Then only one of the ten returned. Jesus said to him, "Arise, go your way. Your faith has made you well." They were all cleansed of leprosy through obedience, but his faith made him complete in his spirit, soul (mind, will, emotions), and body.

14. The high priest's servant (Luke 22:49–51). This was the man whose ear Peter cut off with the sword. There is no mention of faith from anyone; it was an injury, not a disease; and it was acute, not chronic, and caused by someone else. Jesus restored his ear.

15. The nobleman's son (John 4:46–54). The nobleman had faith, but then Jesus reprimanded the people about needing signs and wonders to believe (this would have sent many of us home offended and with a very different outcome). However, the man stayed and continued to plead with Jesus. Jesus said, "Go; your son lives." The man put his trust in what Jesus said and started home; his son lived, and because of this his whole household was saved.

16. The man at the pool of Bethesda sick for thirty-eight years (John 5:1–15).[41] Jesus went to this man. No one had asked, and no faith was required. Jesus asked him if he wanted to be healed; the man did not answer His question but gave all the reasons he wasn't healed. This man had lost hope. Jesus told him, "Rise, take up your bed and walk." But the man had not yet followed this command when he was healed instantly, and then he took up his bed and walked.

17. The man blind from birth (John 9:1–41) The disciples were more worried about why the man was blind, but Jesus took the man, spat, made clay, and put it over his eyes. Then He told the man, "Go, wash in the pool of Siloam." He was healed as he washed in the pool.

---

[40] Scripture quotations for this story are taken from the NKJV.

[41] Scripture quotation for this story is taken from the NKJV.

These stories should give us faith and hope that no healing is beyond Jesus! Jesus only did what He saw the Father do, and He did it by the power of the Holy Spirit (His first miracles were not recorded until after the Holy Spirit came upon Him). Also remember that Jesus' death and resurrection forgave every sin and healed every sickness and every disease, according to 1 Peter 2:24; Psalm 103:1–5; Isaiah 53:3–5. That same Holy Spirit that was in Jesus while on earth is at some level alive in every believer. If you want more, you just need to ask.

Remember, just because so-and-so got healed in a particular way, that doesn't mean that your healing will be manifested in the same way. Ask God! He will show you, because to stand successfully you need *rhema*, and then faith comes! Doctors use different medications based on the individual case, because every person is different, and one thing doesn't work on everybody. The same is true spiritually when it comes to healing. There is no formula; only God knows each case, the faith level of that person, and what works for them. That's why we must ask and then follow what the Holy Spirit says!

Pray and ask God to show you which Scripture passage to apply to your situation. Then ask Him to show you what could be preventing the manifestation of healing. The bottom line is that we live by faith in God through the Holy Spirit's power. I tell you there is nothing more precious than His heart, and getting to know Him is far more precious to me than anything He can give me. However, I couldn't always say that.

Final Thoughts on Our Role in Healing

It matters who our friends are and where we go to church. We need to be a part of a Body of Christ that knows kingdom principles, are actively seeking the heart of God, know how to pray according to God's Word, and expect healings, miracles, signs, and wonders to happen today. If that is not where you are, start searching, because God is bringing forth a remnant, and they are popping up all over the world. Remember, you probably won't match up theologically with every single person, pastor, or leader, but be sure they are preaching the Gospel Jesus preached.

Be teachable, and work with Him to get rid of wrong teachings and wrong beliefs. Believe that He can and will do it more wholly and more completely that we can even imagine. Kineo Ministry Training Center has classes, possibly in a church near you, and they also have an online program. Get to know the God you serve, and learn His heart; learn His heart especially for you. He will change your life and your world, if you invite Him in and then allow Him to reign. Get in the Word; wake up and talk with God every day, because if you begin your day with God, it just tends to go better (or maybe you just don't notice the bad things as much). I heard Roberts Liardon say, "God's always first, if He can just get somebody to believe that with Him."

> Have you need of healing? Pray to God in the name of Jesus Christ to remove the diseases. Command it to leave, as you would sin. Assert your divine authority and refuse to have it. Jesus purchased your freedom from sickness as He purchased your freedom from sin. . . . Therefore, mankind has a right to health, as he has a right to deliverance from sin. If you do not have it, it is because you are being cheated out of your inheritance. It belongs to you. In the name of Jesus Christ, go after it and get it. If your faith is weak, call for those who believe, and to whom the prayer of faith and the ministry of healing has been committed.[42]

[42] John G. Lake, quoted in Roberts Liardon, ed., *The Collected Works of John G. Lake*, 508.

God has been saying the same thing since the beginning, and ever since Jesus lived, a handful of people in each generation has caught His heart concerning healing. I pray we will be one of those few in this generation.

CHAPTER 8

One Last Thing

I KNOW THE title of this chapter may seem vague, but from the beginning I knew there was supposed to be a chapter 8 in this book. What I didn't know is what information the Lord wanted to bring with this chapter, which is why the title gives no clue. This chapter will not be for the faint of heart, but "if you have faith the size of a mustard seed, you will say to this mountain . . ."[43] If you are ready to begin speaking to what seem like impossible circumstances and take a health journey with me that spans three decades, please keep reading.

I have prayed diligently about what to include here, and the guidance He gave came from what I thought would be another book. He told me to share my personal story of my fight with obesity and His healing that would begin on the inside but result in physical change. Sharing this story with the billions of people that I hope will read this book is terrifying to my flesh, my emotions, and my pride. Since the latter needs to die anyway, here we go—the story of my lifelong struggle with weight and all that struggle brings.

Obesity is a disease for which there are no easy answers. I had been obese all of my adult life, and yet I still judged others for it, because mine wasn't caused by hiding cookies and tubs of ice cream

---

43 Matthew 17:20.

(though there have been some pints here and there). I did not see it as a disease; the medical community does not treat it as a disease, and there is shame attached to this disease unlike any other. God was about to deal with my wrong belief about obesity and how He saw it no differently than He does any other disease. Obesity is an epidemic and is not only a physical issue but also a spiritual one. It brings with it shame, guilt, and hatred of the body, which then brings about disease and death. It comes from lies and wrong beliefs from the enemy, and more recently the enemy has us celebrating fat to mask this lie from the pits of hell.

I once heard someone say, "Don't love your bondage so much that you make it ornamental." I immediately thought of the "fat is fabulous" movement sweeping the country, and how we are trying to decorate something that is killing us. I am not saying you should not dress yourself as well as you can, but while dressing the body, realize you need God's healing for your body and deliverance from your destructions (see Psalm 107:20). Obesity is a bondage, a disease that needs healing, and it mostly stems from trauma, where deliverance is needed. We know it is bondage because it limits the places we go, it limits the movement of the body, it brings with it other diseases, and finally, it is a stumbling block to others. However, I have good news, because "where the Spirit of the Lord is, there is liberty [freedom]."[44] God is still in the healing business, the deliverance business, and He loves us right where we are. Scripture tells us that our "bodies [are] a living sacrifice"[45] and "the temple of the Holy Spirit,"[46] and since they are such, we need to care for our bodies.

The new foodie movement is also tactic of the enemy and a path to destruction, because it keeps people focused on satisfying the flesh. When we eat food more than just to sustain the body, it

---

[44] 2 Corinthians 3:17.

[45] Romans 12:1 NKJV.

[46] 1 Corinthians 6:19 NKJV.

places the flesh above the spirit, dulling our ability to hear God. Remember that the enemy came to Jesus and tempted Him with the idea of food. Paul tells us in 1 Corinthians 6:12–13 that everything was permissible but not everything was beneficial, and we are not to be enslaved to anything. He explains that food is for the stomach and the stomach for food, and there will come a day when God will do away with both. A foodie is constantly planning, watching, and learning about food, where to eat, how to cook it, and so on. However, this path leads us to focus on flesh and not on our spirit. Anytime we place anything above God, we make that thing an idol, and worshiping idols is a sin no matter how you try to dress them. In this case, the idol is the spirit of gluttony. According to Philippians 3:19 (NLT), "They are headed for destruction. Their god is their appetite, they brag about shameful things, and they think only about this life here on earth." It's the devil's way of dulling the spirit. John 6:27 tells us not to pursue food that feeds the body as our main goal; instead, we should pursue the food that lasts for eternal life, the food Jesus provided. He is the Bread of Life.

The Lord teaches us to fast in order to consecrate our bodies. If you have ever fasted, you know that you begin to hear God clearer as the days go on. Eventually, the body stops talking, and it is no longer a struggle. Food feeds the flesh, and when our flesh is out of control, it interferes with our ability to hear the Lord. That is exactly what the enemy wants. The Lord showed me that anything that negatively affects my rising early to be with Him is a choice of that thing over Him. When I eat things that I know will make me lethargic the next day, I am choosing food over God. Staying up too late watching TV is choosing entertainment over Him. Here I am, thirty-five years after being labeled obese, sharing the good, the bad, and the ugly of my journey to freedom.

I will begin with verbal curses that were spoken over me as a child; I was told no one would ever love me because I was fat. These words would create a battle in me about food, what to eat, what not to eat, when to eat, when not to eat. Dieting children create bad associations with food, and this causes damage that takes years to repair, short of God intervening sooner. It does not matter who said or did these things to me, except that it was someone I looked up to at one point (and would again, as the Lord healed those places of hurt).

Even as a little girl, I was compared to the other little girls around me. I was already comparing myself because I knew I wasn't like them. I knew I was different because the adults in my life were continually pointing out the differences. By high school, when most girls were in a size 2 to 4, wearing their Jordache or Gloria Vanderbilt jeans, I was a size 9, wearing Lee's or Levi's that were handed down. I was playing football with boys in the street, and I had no desire to be a girl; I wasn't built like one, or at least that is the lie I bought into. I was teased at school, and I thought I was huge, but I told myself that at least I wasn't like this person or that person. Comparison is a trap of the enemy; it is never a good idea for any reason!

I dropped out of high school and was preparing for my first son, right as complications arose. I was already considered fat, and then I became pregnant and was told not to leave the house (except for doctor appointments) because of a heart condition and the heat wave that was occurring in Georgia. I gained eighty-five pounds with that pregnancy, and my greatest fear had come upon me. What that person had said all those years ago, and what I thought about myself, was now true.

Fast-forward two years. When I was pregnant with my second son, I actually gained no weight, but was still carrying the eighty-five pounds I had gained from my first pregnancy, in addition to the twenty pounds I had gained while dating my hubby. Now I was 105 pounds overweight, and I was only eighteen years old. (However, I learned to reject the BMI chart, because it doesn't fit every body type.) I don't like being compared to others; I was made to be different, and it took me years to figure out that I love being the me that God created.

Now my husband and I were stationed in Germany, and I was told that I could not have more children, because I had a growth on my only ovary (I had lost one when Christopher was born), and they were going to have to remove the growth. I had always wanted three children, and I still did not have that elusive girl I so badly desired (for all the wrong reasons). I began to pray and ask God to allow me one more child, and though it actually took six months, I conceived my last son. To some people, six months will not seem like a long time, but six months seemed like an eternity to my nineteen-year-old self. We lived just outside the military base, and I would frequently walk down the mountain into the city of Wertheim to shop and enjoy the area. I had a toddler on my arm, an infant on my front, and one in my body. With all this activity, you would think I would easily lose weight, but that didn't happen. One day, while my regular doctor was away, I saw another physician. This was a British doctor with the worst bedside manner I have ever seen, to date. I walked into the room, and he said, "You're fat." I was thinking, "And you're rude." Then I noticed on my patient chart the words "morbidly obese." I never saw that doctor again. I gave birth to my third son, and in addition to chasing my children around, I began playing sports again. Even so, no weight loss. By this point I had dieted at least four times in my adult life, and I mean really dieted, without any real results, and I was only twenty years old.

Three years later, I was back in the U.S., and I hadn't eaten at my favorite restaurants in three years. I spent the next few months eating fast food, fried foods, and Southern cooking, so you can imagine what happened. I was still 125 pounds over an ideal weight, and now I was gaining more. I gained about fifty more pounds before it was over. I snapped out of the fast-food craze when someone told me that all I talked about was food, and they were right. I dreamed about it, planned it, prepared it, and ate it. All of this weight remained with me, along with the guilt and the thoughts that I would always be this way, that I was an embarrassment to my family and to God. The whole time I was beating myself up, I was also declaring these things out loud: "You are fat; look at you"; "You're disgusting"; "That person was right"; "If you eat that it will make you fat"; "This food is bad for you"; and so on. Those are just some of the curses I spoke over myself. That doesn't even include the additional thoughts I had about myself and food that proved to be a problem later, as God showed me the issues.

Let's fast-forward to the year 2000. Up until this point, I had only done what I was taught and told and what my natural responses were to stress. In 2000, I had just come from the life-changing mission trip to Zambia, I was preparing for nursing school, and I was seeking the Lord with all my heart. One day, in the year 2000 (I don't know the exact date, because the younger me thought I would always remember it, and I didn't write it down), I went to a night church service somewhere north of Atlanta. It was a little white church building across the street from a set of railroad tracks, where some people in our church knew the pastor. The speaker that night was Mama Greene, a little African American lady in spiked heels, who had fire in her hands and the Word in her mouth—she was anointed and had supernatural heat coming from her hands. I am still amazed by the way she moved around that stage in those heels, as she had to be eighty years old at the time.

This is where faith comes in. I had been seeking the Lord about my weight, and I had been eating better and following the Holy Spirit's instruction for what to eat. During worship that night, I closed my eyes and was just focused on the Lord when suddenly I began to feel lighter in my body, and then I began to see the weight fall off in the Spirit. I was amazed and excited! Then I opened my eyes, and to my shock, I was still the same in the natural flesh. I am telling you, I felt it fall off, but it was still there. I looked back to the Lord, confused about what just happened, and I heard Him tell me, "The weight will fall off as you dance before Me." For the next couple years, I danced around the house while cleaning and worshiping the Lord, and I danced as best I could in a crowded choir loft. I loved to dance anyway, and now I had even more reasons to do it. The weight did begin to come off, and people began to ask me what I was doing. I told them that this was the Lord; I was not dieting or on any exercise program. I was only following the Holy Spirit's guidance.

This was about the time that bariatric surgeries really began to climb in numbers, and I personally knew of three people who had these surgeries. Their results varied, but one has kept it off all these years, one died from surgical complications within days, and one continued to struggle with weight. I was approached multiple times about bariatric surgery; as a person in my twenties with no other health issues, I was a perfect candidate. Each time I would just say, "No, the Lord is going to take care of it." Again, I will say, we can only follow where our own faith will take us! I am not condemning anyone's choices; I am just sharing some of the stories I have seen and heard through the years. The Lord will use whatever avenues we will allow Him or that we have faith in.

By 2005, life had worn me down. My husband had just been placed into a nursing home, I had been working twelve-hour night shifts, and I was consuming one meal at about 1 a.m. every morning in the ICU. By the time I got home, I was too tired to eat, and when I woke up it was time to return to work, so there was no time to eat. I had lost sight of God's promise concerning my weight. I started seeking out a surgeon, and I already knew the right one. I proceeded to go through all the steps required for surgical clearance, which included a psychological evaluation that would turn out to be a literal lifesaver. Remember my major depressive disorder? Well, this therapist was part of God's answer to get me through it until I could receive a miraculous healing in that area. After that evaluation was done, I was approved and ready for my surgical date.

Although I had forgotten God's promise, He had not, and that date would never come. What happened next snapped me back into reality, or out of it, depending on which reality you want to consider (the natural or the spiritual). I received a phone call from a close friend whom I had not heard from in two years (she had been going through difficulties too). She began the conversation as though we had been talking about this subject already, because God had been talking to her about it on my behalf. She said, "Hey, what are you doing?" I thought that was the conversation starter, but she did not mean it the way I thought. I said, "Nothing." She said, "No, I mean what are you planning? And whatever it is, God said, 'It's not for you.' " I began to tell her about the surgical plans and how I thought this was an answer to my prayer now, since I had tried everything else. (Notice how I no longer recalled God's words to me that night; I was thinking He changed His mind.) We talked for a while and caught up, and then after we hung up, I began to talk with God about it—as if He hadn't been clear enough. I was sad, but then the more I thought, the more I began to realize that if the Lord was saying no, then I would have no spiritual covering and the devil could cause me real harm, even death. I had seen enough as a nurse already to realize I wasn't going into surgery of any kind without God. I called the surgeon's office to cancel the surgery, and when my friend who worked there answered the phone, she said, "Oh, thank God! I didn't feel you were supposed to have this surgery." I said, "What?! You didn't say anything!" She said, "I didn't feel like I could since I work here, but I was praying God would show you." However, even though I had received this revelation, I still did not remember God's word to dance before Him, nor the weight loss in the Spirit that had occurred.

In 2007, I was blessed with a seven-day trip to Canyon Ranch in Massachusetts. Please allow me to indulge for a moment, because this story shows how God cares about even the little things in our lives. Once I knew I was going to Canyon Ranch at Christmastime,

I began to ask God for snow. I had only ever dreamed of a white Christmas, because we didn't have those in Georgia. Well, the night I arrived, it snowed seventeen inches! I looked out my window and saw the most perfect snowcapped Christmas tree I had ever seen, as if God put it there just for me. I sat on the end of the bed smiling from ear to ear, with tears running down my face, knowing only God and I knew the secret. It was even more amazing when the locals told me, "It never snows like this this early in the season; this usually happens in February." I inwardly rejoiced and chuckled with God. I then popped on my winter clothes and headed outside to build a snowman. The only problem was that the snow did not have ice in it; it was powder, and it would not hold together. I did finally get a snowman built, but he was tiny and on a park bench, where the snow had melted and refrozen. Thanks for allowing me to share that memory; it always brings a smile to my face and reminds me of His faithfulness.

While I was learning how to better care for my body, God was showing me that He cared for my dreams and thoughts, no matter how small. I wasn't there for the snow (that was just the Lord's bonus), but I was there to learn why I wasn't losing weight. By this time, I had learned how to make better food choices, my intake was more on the normal side, and I did not live a dormant lifestyle, yet I was still "morbidly obese." There had to be a natural cause, right? I had appointments and tests with naturopaths, herbalists, and other functional health experts, during which they discovered that my body was in starvation mode, and probably had been for some time. Ironically, this gave me hope, because that meant we could fix it. When our bodies are in starvation mode, they will store everything we eat, even healthy foods, into fat cells. This is then used by the body for energy consumption when there is a lack of food available. Those 1:00 a.m. meals, which definitely were not healthy, were being stored because my body was burning more calories than I was providing it. This was when I realized that the old adage, "Calories in, calories out," was not the whole story for weight loss. I had created this mess through a lack of knowledge (there is a Scripture passage about that), poor habits, and stress. Now I knew what was wrong. The specialists had created a plan for me, and it was time to execute it. However, focusing on this proved more difficult for me than I thought, considering all that was happening with Christopher, Mike, and my oldest son in an actual war zone.

At this point in the story, it was now 2009, and I weighed about four hundred pounds. I had changed cities and now lived in Athens, Georgia—the Classic City, home of my favorite sports team. I was severely depressed, and if something didn't change, I was not going to make it. My faith was far from me, and that car conversation with my son that shook me to my core had happened just a few months earlier. I began to search online for a trainer. I needed help, and I needed it now, because I had to lose weight. If I fixed the weight, I would feel better, and all my other problems would be doable (at least, that's what I told myself). God, in His mercy, intervened and took me right where I needed to be. I found a person who owned a small local gym; I called him and explained my situation, and he promised me he could help. I came to the gym, looked around, and said, "What the *(bleep)* do you expect me to be able to do here?" (I told you my faith had failed me.) This gym ran a program called CrossFit and was set up for training college students and athletes. He promised again that he could help, and he would tailor a workout that I could actually do. He asked me how I found him, so I told him what I searched online, but when we recreated the exact search, his name did not come up. No matter what we typed in the search bar, unless you used the term *CrossFit* (which I did not know of yet), neither his gym nor his name showed up. I said that it must have been God who brought me here then, and with that I went home.

For the next nine months, there was lots of crying, cursing, sweating, and believe it or not, laughing. This man, who had become a close friend, had me walking, jumping rope, lifting weights, and developing a love/hate relationship with things like kettle bells, wallball, and the rowing machine. While I was developing this relationship with the gym, I was also resetting my metabolism to get it out of starvation mode and dropping weight weekly. I began swimming daily, and before long I was swimming a mile a day and was even preparing to compete in some weightlifting competitions. My focus was 100 percent all in on my health and wellness, which may not sound bad until you realize I had tossed out God with everything else. In those nine months, I lost almost one hundred pounds (one month I lost twenty-five pounds), gained a ton of confidence, and started living again. The only problem was that I was not living unto the Lord, but unto the world. All those worldly things I thought I had missed having children so young—going to bars, hanging out with friends, and traveling—were now doable with my children grown. I could take my love/hate relationship with CrossFit anywhere, and now it was popular all over the world, so off I went as a travel nurse until 2012. Nevertheless, God continued to speak to me through others, even while I was stepping in and out of communication with Him. I knew what was right, but I thought I was entitled to these experiences I had missed—right? (The correct answer is no!) Thank God, He did not leave me there, and He guided me home.

In 2012, God intervened again and saved me from my destructive self by bringing Todd into the picture. We met and were married within six weeks, because we both knew the Lord had brought us together. I began gaining weight at ridiculous speed despite no real lifestyle changes, except that I had stopped swimming. I was now living in a new area where no one knew me, and they did not listen when I would tell them I gained fifteen pounds in two weeks. Only one hundred pounds and about nine months later did they finally figure out there was a problem, and it was hyperthyroidism.

I have to explain something here, because there are two main categories of thyroid disorders, *hyper* and *hypo*, and the symptoms are the opposite of each other. Hypothyroidism has symptoms such as hair loss, weight gain, constipation, sensitivity to cold, dry skin, and fatigue, while symptoms of hyperthyroidism include anxiousness, fast heart rate, weight loss, muscle weakness, irritability, and trouble sleeping. They discovered I had hyperthyroidism because I went into atrial fibrillation, and now someone was paying attention. The only puzzle was how on earth did my hyperthyroidism cause weight gain, when it was supposed to cause weight loss! Now I was angry, because not only did I have heart issues that prevented me from working out, but I also felt terrible, and I had gained every pound I had worked so hard to lose. When I asked the endocrinologist about it, he said 2 percent of patients with thyroid disease will have symptoms from both sides (insert a sigh and an eye roll). My body had betrayed me, and I should have recognized this as a spiritual issue, but I was not there yet. You already know the struggles of the next few years with my son and the atrial fibrillation battle from previous chapters, but there is so much more to this story. The main idea here is to show how God continued to be faithful in His promises; while He still allowed me to make my own choices, even the bad ones, He would always call me back to Himself. It is not too late to turn back to Him!

Another thing that caught my attention regarding my weight was a documentary about using food as medicine. In 2014, I was watching this documentary when I saw this healthy, fit man telling how he used to weigh over four hundred pounds. He had my attention, as he shared that he had no surgeries, did not go on any special diets, and lived an active lifestyle, but he still weighed four hundred pounds, and no one could understand why. I thought to myself, "Hey, he is like me!" He shared how he discovered that his thinking was all wrong, so he changed his thinking and by doing so he changed his body. From what I could see, he was doing all this from a non-Christian meditation standpoint, but I bought his book anyway. Something inside me resonated with this, and I knew that "mind over matter" was real, because I had seen it with patients. I had seen a patient die within minutes of a diagnosis that should not have killed them immediately, and I had seen patients pull through who should have died, and they weren't even awake to think. From a medical standpoint, I knew that if a patient was afraid they would die in surgery, they were 25 to 30 percent more likely to die. I knew that the mind controls the signals, and if we could change the signals, we could have a different response. I just needed someone to associate those things with weight. I want to say that I am not negating God moving in these situations. Proverbs 23:7 (KJV) says, "As [a man] thinketh in his heart, so is he," so this principle does work, regardless of belief in God.

For the next several years I was unable to do CrossFit training due to atrial fibrillation, and I abhorred walking, so I stopped exercising. However, I did start listening to the meditations to reprogram my thinking. The "programming" has to do with the fight-or-flight response that is in our earthly genetic makeup. According to this earthly programming, my body was programmed to store fat under stress, while others are programmed to lose fat under stress. But I am part of Christ's genetics now, so this earthly programming has been overridden by God.

I had lost twenty-five or so pounds when I realized that my thinking about this was even more wrong than I thought. Though twenty-five pounds doesn't seem like much when you need to lose 225, it should still be celebrated. I could not keep ignoring the present success and always be looking ahead, or I was going to miss my entire life. When Chris died, I gained back the twenty-five pounds again, and those genetics, along with the enemy, were screaming back at me. I have already discussed the battle within me during this time, so I will skip to the next event that God used to speak to me.

In 2019, I had reunited with the Lord, and He began to teach me how to eat. He wanted me to eat natural foods, things that grew in the ground, things not made by man but by God. While exercising within the CrossFit community, I had adopted a gluten-free lifestyle, and my body began rejecting bread where it had never experienced issues before (again, our bodies will match what we believe, as Proverbs 23:7 says). That all changed when I took a trip to the Amish country in Ohio, where I was able to eat any bread and grains they served without issue. I realized it wasn't gluten that was the problem, so what was it? I discovered through research that it was the processing methods and chemicals creating all the issues. I also later began having issues with GF products because of how overprocessed they are. I began to pray about what to do. Then I remembered a woman at our church years ago who ground her own flour, and I loved her breads. I felt that the Lord was leading me to grind my own grains and make my own bread, and that I needed to stop believing the gluten-free, dairy-free lies I had bought into. The latter part was more difficult than I thought it would be due to my medical mind. I was researching and learning about how to grind flour and what supplies I would need when 2020 happened. At that time there was not a mill grinder to be found, nor any other bread supplies, so I was unable to begin.

Later that year, I was listening to a minister on YouTube when he said something that caught both my attention and my spirit. He said, "If you have something you have battled all your life, done everything you know to do in the natural, and it hasn't changed, it's time to let it go and give it to God." I immediately thought of my weight battle, so I sat with the Lord and gave it to Him. I considered the obvious miracle in all of this, and that was that I had none of these diseases. The medical providers were always amazed at my lab work; I did not have high blood pressure, diabetes, high cholesterol, or any other diseases that ran in my family. The Lord had kept me in health despite my weight, and I was to celebrate this body that so graciously carried me all these years without breaking down. Suddenly I was aware that this weight was not a natural issue at all; it was a spiritual one, and it was an attack on me to prevent me from healing the sick. I had helped many patients claim their victory over disease, understand food and their bodies, and have hope for better health. God had gifted me in nursing and gave me insight into my patients, but an obese practitioner appears like a hypocrite, and I felt that! I loved working with patients and their families, but my heart's desire was to lay hands on the sick and see them recover. This weight was a tactic of the enemy to keep me too embarrassed to step into my calling of God.

Unknowingly, I had made agreements with lies from the enemy, ones that I still believed in. Now this was all beginning to make some sense. I had done everything the experts said, and yet I never reached a real goal or fit in the "acceptable weight" category. I had battled this since childhood, and my parents didn't have sweets in our home; we also didn't eat take-out or fast food because we were poor. I had developed bad spiritual habits, and I was cursing myself and my food with my thoughts and words. I would eat things I had just declared I shouldn't eat, which was creating doublemindedness in me. I began to read Scripture passages concerning food, and I discovered gluttony wasn't just overeating, but it was eating the "delicacies of kings" (see Proverbs 23:13), which would be tasty but have no nutritional value (sounds like the U.S. food market). The Lord went on to teach me how to watch my thoughts and my words and to take these thoughts captive based on 2 Corinthians 10:4–6. When we say, "I should not eat this," and then we eat it anyway, we are not acting in faith, and that which is not of faith is sin (see Romans14:23), which then gives the devil access to us. When we speak over our food, "This is going to show up on my thighs later," we are cursing what God has already blessed, and according to Numbers 23:8, this is not something we should do. I could see how God was teaching me, reprogramming me, and healing me from the inside out. Although I still had yet to remember the promise from 2000 in the little white church building, I was working with God to place my body under His control. I started being mindful of my thoughts and any agreements with lies of the enemy, and I began speaking to my body to accept the food God had created us to eat. I was speaking to my immune system not to create any histamine response (overactive or allergic response) to any foods, animals, or plants God created. I was feeding my spirit with the biblical teachings of those who had evidence of walking in divine health. This was all preparation, but God was about to blow my mind, and I clearly wasn't ready for that.

For years, I had believed that if man's inventions for weight loss could produce rapid results, then my God could do better than that; after all, He created the body. Each time I was tempted to try man's methods for weight loss, the Lord would stop me. However, even my wild imagination about how God could do this didn't prepare me for what He said next. On February 25, 2021, as I sat with the Lord talking about the truths He had been teaching me, He spoke to me and said, "Ask Me for your body. Ask Me for the 145-pound body I showed you in 2000 and that you felt happen." I said okay, and I remembered Jesse Duplantis's story of his mom praying for his teeth because she couldn't afford braces, and the Lord straightened his teeth. My faith was growing, but unfortunately, I wasn't quite there. As I was making my list of body "issues" I wanted gone, I thought about Sarah, Abraham's wife, and how even in her old age the king of Gerar wanted her as a concubine. That meant she must have been beautiful and youthful in appearance, so I wasn't being vain in asking for physical things. God brought Naaman to my memory, and how He restored his skin to being like that of a child (see 2 Kings 6:14). With this thought, I added more items to my list. Now, I know some will scream, "Name it and claim it," but God asked, and I had already learned that God is a God of details, and vague prayers don't get specific answers. Then I stopped to think about that lost ovary; I didn't need the ovary any longer, but I still wanted my body whole again, because that is the way He created me. Was I supposed to put that on the list, or was that too much or wrong to ask for, since I didn't need it anymore? I knew that God promised that divine health is part of our salvation, and it was already paid for by Jesus, so I wanted it all. Right in the midst of this internal dilemma, God said, "Seriously, that's the belief you're having trouble with? All the rest is okay, but that's too much?" I laughed, and then He showed me Matthew 6:9–13, and I understood: "On earth as it is in heaven." In heaven I will be whole and perfect, so I declare now, on earth as it is in heaven! However, my next prayer proved what a lack of faith I had at that time. I prayed that for the next six months to a year that God would prepare me and show me, that He would grow my faith so I could believe and receive such a miracle. I wished I hadn't been cautious and that I had only believed, but it was too late now; I had already discounted the instant miracle. God is gracious in mercy and slow to anger, so He has gone at my pace on this, which has been slow and steady. This promise, however, did prevent me from being tempted by other methods of weight loss; even though they work for others, I knew that was not His desire for me. Do you know how difficult it is to hang on to a "crazy" promise when others around you are being delivered through other methods? Do you know how difficult it is to not lose hope, to be that radical person who believes when it is naturally impossible? Well, God did, so He sent me reinforcements. I knew that God was telling me what He was going to do was not going to be a process or gradual weight loss; it was going to occur suddenly. I am a visual person, so I needed something to look at as a reminder, so I went online to Belk's and started looking for a pair of jeans. I knew that with my build, at 145 pounds I would be about a 7/8. And there they were, Gloria Vanderbilt jeans, on sale for $10, and the only size available was an 8! I bought them and hung them on the back of my closet door so that they would be the last thing I see every night before bed. I didn't tell a soul but pondered in my heart until He instructed me to share.

I began reading every *God's Generals* book I could get my hands on. I needed to read about other radical miracles to help my faith and dispel unbelief. I read of a woman who lost two hundred pounds when A. A. Allen laid hands on her, while everyone watched. God confirmed this word to me time and time again, and then, just when I thought I had a grasp on it, He upped the ante. Ministers kept popping up in my YouTube feed—people I had forgotten of, never heard, or never seen before. This occurred while I watched only specific ministers, so I wasn't searching for them, but these new people were a little more radical in their faith and had amazing testimonies. Then the Lord brought me Amy Freudiger's testimony of being healed overnight, and I knew that was what the Lord was telling me. The "suddenly" would happen as I slept, so I began getting excited, and every night I took a "before" photo for proof. Then the Lord reminded me not to have a backup plan, and He instructed me to donate all the clothes that I was not currently wearing (this included those containers of previous sizes). I had some cute and nice things in there, but I was preparing for my future, not looking back. However, I still needed help for my faith, because this was more radical than anything I had ever seen, and the implications were mind-boggling. I know how all this sounds, and I wouldn't be sharing if God had not instructed me to do so. Every day, I would wake up sort of disappointed, and then I would decide I wasn't going to focus on this so much; I felt I was allowing it to get me out of sorts. During this time, He did have me share this with my husband and two close friends. The Lord showed one friend the end result in a dream, and the other (the one from the surgeon's office) confirmed it immediately. I wasn't crazy, and as time went on with no physical evidence, the Lord would continue to send people with words to confirm His word to me to keep me encouraged.

Since the promise, I have taken those jeans, a t-shirt, and accessories with me whenever I traveled, because I didn't want to be caught unprepared. However, this was Kineo year I graduation, and those jeans wouldn't be appropriate (though I don't think anyone would have said anything), so I purchased a cute blouse and slacks to take to the hotel with me. I was unusually excited about this night, and I went to sleep with lots of anticipation for the next day. That night, as I slept, it happened again: I felt the weight melt away. This time it was in a dream, and in the dream I had felt the Holy Spirit hover over me and the weight literally melt away. I was shocked, first in the dream and then when I woke up and saw it had not changed in the natural. Even though it had not manifested, I was still on cloud nine. I had a dress I was wearing for graduation, making sure it met the criteria for walking across the stage as well as what we used to call "Church of God safe" (meaning that you would still be covered up if you ended up on the floor in carpet time with the Holy Spirit).

Now I did end up on the carpet in front of hundreds (possibly millions) of people, but not because of the Holy Spirit. Yes, I tripped and fell face-first on the stage in a dress, my worst nightmare (which was the issue). I had tried not to think of those stairs, and I rebuked those thoughts of falling in front of the whole church (not even thinking about TV). But God showed me later that I had concerned myself with this many times in church, so those seeds were already planted. He really means for us to "[take] every thought captive" (2 Corinthians 10:5), and this was a clear lesson in why. Some of the Kineo students told me it was a graceful fall and that I handled it with elegance (that was definitely God, because elegance has never been one of my traits). Funny enough, my first thought, after finding out I remained covered, was, "Well, that's one way to become known around the world!" There were now millions of witnesses to my current size, so when the miracle manifests, there should be little doubt about how it happened. Later, God told me, "I cannot have your identity connected to an event, and I cannot have your identity connected to your body. Your identity must be found in Me and Me alone." That would be the focus of the next year and a half.

Twice now I have felt this weight gone from my body, and now I began having dreams and even visions during church of me in my jeans ministering to others. Later, in August 2021, I felt it again while I was dreaming, in between sleep and waking. In this dream, I told God that I was saying yes to any way He wanted to manifest the healing paid for by Jesus. I did not want to lock Him into my idea of how He should accomplish it, although I knew He had impressed upon me "suddenly" and then "overnight." Within the dream, right as I said, "Yes, Lord, any way You desire," I felt the Holy Spirit moving up and down my body three times. Two times there was no change, and I would look and see everything was still the same, but on the third time, I saw the manifestation. So now I am expectantly awaiting the third visitation of the Spirit, as I feel God throwing me nuggets to keep my faith high.

February 25, 2022, marked one year, and nothing had changed externally, but so much had changed internally. The Lord had given me a heart for others with weight problems, and He taught me that it didn't matter if the disease was self-inflicted; it was still covered by the cross. These lessons God was teaching me came almost daily. His voice became louder and louder, and most of the time I was tuned in loud and clear. But we know the enemy isn't going to just roll over and allow us to rise up, which is why you read about all those battles in my body during this time and the time of writing this book.

The enemy's goal during all this was to get my eyes off Jesus, off the promise given, because if he could get me to doubt or to give up in the waiting, then he would win. But God is always ahead of the devil, so if we pay attention to the Holy Spirit, we will be made aware of the enemy's tactics. I did stop praying every day for the manifestation, but that was because there was one day in which the Lord instructed me on what to do and how to pray, and it brought complete knowledge that it was done. No more praying would be required, so I just began thanking Him for it after that day. Here we are, just days away from 2023, and again my anticipation has been growing, not only for this miracle but also because there is something stirring in the Spirit concerning the next year. The month of December has been all about consecration and crucifying my flesh, ending the year well and ridding myself of anything that isn't of God. As of this day, December 26, 2022, the manifestation has yet to occur in the natural, but my faith has never been more sure. Some mornings I wake up totally unaware of the body in which I currently reside. It sounds strange, but it's true; it just isn't my focus any longer. I can now honestly say that I am thankful He didn't do it before, because I can see how much my pride would have increased and how I would have fallen pretty fast or done some damage to others. I can see the issues in me He has been working to remove and the areas of flesh that I needed to get under submission of His Spirit. I can see how my eyes were focused on the wrong areas. He has had me share this entire story prior to the manifestation to assist in killing my flesh. I cannot be worried about what others will think; I only need to follow Him. I would have kept this all to myself, but He chose to end this book in anticipation of the manifestation of a miracle promised almost twenty-three years ago. This is a "declare it from the mountaintop" moment. He is faithful, and we need only believe.

Appendix A

Scriptures Concerning Healing,
Your Authority, and Faith

Genesis 20:17 (NLT)

Then Abraham prayed to God, and God healed Abimelech, his wife, and his female servants, so they could have children.

Exodus 15:26

And He said, "If you will [listen carefully] to the voice of the LORD your God, and do what is right in His sight, and [listen] to His commandments, and keep all His statutes, I will put none of the diseases on you which I have put on the Egyptians; for I, the LORD, am your healer."

Exodus 23:25–26

25 But you shall serve the LORD your God, and He will bless your
bread and your water; and I will remove sickness from your midst.
26 There shall be no one miscarrying or barren in your land; I will
fulfill the number of your days.

Deuteronomy 7:14–15

14 You shall be blessed above all peoples; there will be no male or
female barren among you or among your cattle. 15 The LORD will
remove from you all sickness; and He will not put on you any of the
harmful diseases of Egypt which you have known, but He will lay
them on all who hate you.

Deuteronomy 34:7

Although Moses was one hundred and twenty years old when he died, his eye was not dim, nor his vigor abated.

1 Kings 13:6 (NLT)

The king cried out to the man of God, "Please ask the LORD your God to restore my hand again!" So the man of God prayed to the LORD, and the king's hand was restored and he could move it again.

2 Kings 20:1–6 (NKJV)

[1] In those days Hezekiah was sick and near death. And Isaiah the
prophet, the son of Amoz, went to him and said to him, "Thus says
the Lord: 'Set your house in order, for you shall die, and not live.' "

[2] Then he turned his face toward the wall, and prayed to the
Lord, saying, [3] "Remember now, O Lord, I pray, how I have walked
before You in truth and with a loyal heart, and have done what was
good in Your sight." And Hezekiah wept bitterly.

[4] And it happened, before Isaiah had gone out into the middle
court, that the word of the Lord came to him, saying, [5] "Return and
tell Hezekiah the leader of My people, 'Thus says the Lord, the God
of David your father: "I have heard your prayer, I have seen your
tears; surely I will heal you. On the third day you shall go up to the
house of the Lord. [6] And I will add to your days fifteen years. I will
deliver you and this city from the hand of the king of Assyria; and I
will defend this city for My own sake, and for the sake of My servant
David." ' "

Psalm 34:17–20

[17] The righteous cry, and the LORD hears And delivers them out of
all their troubles.

[18] The LORD is near to the brokenhearted And saves those who
are crushed in spirit.

19 Many are the afflictions of the righteous, but the LORD delivers him out of them all.

20 He keeps all his bones, not one of them broken.

Psalm 41:1–3

1 How blessed is he who considers the helpless; The LORD will deliver him in a day of trouble.

2 The LORD will protect him and keep him alive, And he shall be called blessed upon the earth; And do not give him over to the desire of his enemies.

3 The LORD will sustain him upon his sickbed; In his illness, You restore him to health.

Psalm 84:11

For the LORD God is a sun and shield; The LORD gives grace and glory; No good thing does He withhold from those who walk uprightly.

Psalm 103:1–5

1 Bless the LORD, O my soul, And all that is within me, bless His holy name.

2 Bless the LORD, O my soul, And forget none of his benefits;

3 Who pardons all your iniquities, Who heals all your diseases;

4 Who redeems your life from the pit, Who crowns you with lovingkindness and compassion;

5 Who satisfies your years with good things, So that your youth is renewed like the eagle.

Psalm 107:6, 9, 13, 19, 20, 28

6 Then they cried out to the LORD in their trouble; He delivered them out of their distresses. . . .

9 For He has satisfied the thirsty soul, And the hungry soul He has filled with what is good. . . .

[13] Then they cried out to the LORD in their trouble; He saved them out of their distresses. . . .

[19] Then they cried out to the LORD in their trouble; He saved them out of their distresses. . . .

[20] He sent His word and healed them, And delivered them from their destructions. . . .

[28] Then they cried out to the LORD in their trouble, And He brought them out of their distresses.

Proverbs 3:7–8

[7] Do not be wise in your own eyes; fear the LORD and turn away from evil.

[8] It will be healing to your body And refreshment to your bones.

Proverbs 4:20–22

[20] My son, give attention to my words; Incline your ear to my sayings.

[21] Do not let them depart from your sight; Keep them in the midst of your heart.

[22] For they are life to those who find them and health to all their body.

Proverbs 17:22

A joyful heart is good medicine, but a broken spirit dries up the bones.

Isaiah 26:3 (NKJV)

You will keep him in perfect peace, Whose mind is stayed on You, Because he trusts in You.

Isaiah 41:10, 13 (NKJV)

[10] Fear not, for I am with you; Be not dismayed, for I am your God. I will strengthen you, Yes, I will help you, I will uphold you with My righteous right hand. . . .

13 For I, the LORD your God, will hold your right hand, Saying to you, "Fear not, I will help you."

Isaiah 53:5 (NKJV)
But He was wounded for our transgressions, He was bruised for our iniquities; The chastisement for our peace [shalom] was upon Him, And by his stripes we are healed.

Isaiah 55:11 (NKJV)
So shall My word be that goes forth from My mouth; It shall not return to Me void, But it shall accomplish what I please, And it shall prosper in the thing for which I sent it.

Isaiah 61:1–3
1 The Spirit of the Lord GOD is upon me, Because the LORD has anointed me To bring good news to the afflicted; He has sent me to bind up the brokenhearted, To proclaim liberty to captives And freedom to prisoners;
2 To proclaim the favorable year of the LORD And the day of vengeance of our God; To comfort all who mourn,
3 To grant those who mourn in Zion, Giving them a garland instead of ashes, The oil of gladness instead of mourning, The mantle of praise instead of a spirit of fainting. So they will be called oaks of righteousness, The planting of the LORD, that He may be glorified.

Matthew 4:23–24 (NKJV)
23 Jesus went about all Galilee, teaching in their synagogues, preach-
ing the gospel of the kingdom, and healing all kinds of sickness
and all kinds of disease among the people. 24 Then His fame went
throughout all Syria; and they brought to Him all sick people who
were afflicted with various diseases and torments, and those who
were demon-possessed, epileptics, and paralytics; and He healed
them.

Matthew 6:10 (NKJV)
Your kingdom come. Your will be done On earth as it is in heaven.

Matthew 9:22
But Jesus turning and seeing her said, "Daughter, take courage; your faith has made you well."

Matthew 9:35 (NKJV)
Jesus went about all the cities and villages, teaching in their synagogues, preaching the gospel of the kingdom, and healing every sickness and every disease among the people.

Matthew 10:1 (NKJV)
And when [Jesus] had called His twelve disciples to Him, He gave them power over unclean spirits, to cast them out, and to heal all kinds of sickness and all kinds of disease.

Matthew 10:8 (NKJV)
Heal the sick, cleanse the lepers, raise the dead, cast out demons. Freely you have received, freely give.

Matthew 12:15
But Jesus, aware of this, withdrew from there. Many followed Him, and He healed them all.

Matthew 14:14 (NKJV)
And when Jesus went out He saw a great multitude; and He was moved with compassion for them, and healed their sick.

Matthew 14:35–36 (NKJV)
35 And when the men of that place recognized Him, they sent out into all that surrounding region, brought to Him all who were sick,

[36] and begged Him that they might only touch the hem of His garment. And as many as touched it were made perfectly well.

Mark 5:36 (NKJV)
Do not be afraid; only believe.

Mark 9:23
And Jesus said to Him, " 'If you can?' All things are possible to him who believes."

Mark 11:22–24
[22] And Jesus answered saying to them, "Have faith in God. [23] Truly I
say to you, whoever says to this mountain, 'Be taken up and cast into the sea,' and does not doubt in his heart, but believes that what he says is going to happen, it will be granted him.

[24] Therefore I say to you, all things for which you pray and ask, believe that you have received them, and they will be granted you."

Mark 16:17–18 (NKJV)
[17] These signs will follow those who believe: In My name they will
cast out demons; they will speak with new tongues; [18] they will take
up serpents; and if they drink anything deadly, it will by no means hurt them; they will lay hands on the sick, and they will recover.

Luke 4:18 (NKJV)
The Spirit of the LORD is upon Me, Because He has anointed Me to preach the gospel to the poor; He has sent Me to heal the brokenhearted, to proclaim liberty to the captives And recovery of sight to the blind, To set at liberty those who are oppressed.

Luke 4:40 (NKJV)
When the sun was setting, all those who had any that were sick with

various diseases brought them to Him; and He laid His hands on every one of them and healed them.

Luke 6:17–19 (NKJV)

17 And [Jesus] came down with them and stood on a level place with
a crowd of His disciples and a great multitude of people from all
Judea and Jerusalem, and from the seacoast of Tyre and Sidon, who
came to hear Him and be healed of their diseases, 18 as well as those
who were tormented with unclean spirits. And they were healed.
19 And the whole multitude sought to touch Him, for power went
out from Him and healed them all.

Luke 9:1-2 (NKJV)

1Then He called His twelve disciples together and gave them power
and authority over all demons, and to cure diseases. 2He sent them
to preach the kingdom of God, and heal the sick."

Luke 9:56 (NKJV)

For the Son of Man did not come to destroy men's lives but to save them.

Luke 10:19 (NKJV)

Behold, I give you the authority to trample on serpents and scorpions, and over all the power of the enemy, and nothing shall by any means hurt you.

Luke 13:12–13

12 When Jesus saw her, He called her over and said to her, "Woman,
you are freed from your sickness." 13 And He laid His hands on her;
and immediately she was made erect again and began glorifying
God.

Luke 17:6

And the Lord said, "If you had faith like a mustard seed, you would say to this mulberry tree, 'Be uprooted and be planted by the sea'; and it would obey you."

John 10:10 (NKJV)

The thief does not come except to steal, and to kill, and to destroy. I have come that they may have life, and that they may have it more abundantly.

John 14:12–14

12 Truly, truly, I say to you, he who believes in Me, the works that I
do, he will do also; and greater works than these he will do; because
I go to the Father. 13 Whatever you ask in My name, that will I do,
so that the Father may be glorified in the Son. 14 If you ask Me
anything in My name, I will do it.

John 15:7

If you abide in Me, and My words abide in you, ask whatever you wish, and it will be done for you.

John 16:23-24 (NKJV)

23And in that day you will ask Me nothing. Most assuredly I say to
you, whatever you ask of the Father in My name He will give you.
24 Until now you have asked nothing in My name. Ask, and you will
receive, that your joy may be full.

Acts 5:15–16

15 They even carried the sick out into the streets and laid them on
cots and pallets, so that when Peter came by at least his shadow
might fall on any one of them. 16 Also the people from the cities
in the vicinity of Jerusalem were coming together, bringing people

who were sick or afflicted with unclean spirits, and they were all being healed.

Acts 10:38
You know of Jesus of Nazareth, how God anointed Him with the Holy Spirit and with power, and how He went about doing good and healing all who were oppressed by the devil, for God was with Him.

Romans 8:11 (NKJV)
11 But if the Spirit of Him who raised Jesus from the dead lives in you, He who raised Christ from the dead will give life [zoe] to your mortal bodies through His Spirit who dwells in you.

2 Corinthians 1:20 (NKJV)
For all the promises of God in Him are Yes, and in Him Amen, to the glory of God through us.

2 Corinthians 3:17 (NKJV)
Now the Lord is the Spirit; and where the Spirit of the Lord is, there is liberty.

Ephesians 3:20 (NKJV)
Now to Him who is able to do exceedingly abundantly above all that we ask or think, according to the power that works in us.

Philippians 4:19 (NKJV)
And my God shall supply all your need according to His riches in glory by Christ Jesus.

1 Thessalonians 5:23
Now may the God of peace Himself sanctify you entirely; and may

your spirit, soul, and body, be preserved complete, without blame at the coming of our Lord Jesus Christ.

2 Timothy 1:7 (NKJV)
For God has not given us a spirit of fear, but of power and of love and of a sound mind.

Hebrews 6:12 (NKJV)
Do not become [slothful], but imitate those who through faith and patience inherit the promises.

Hebrews 13:8 (NKJV)
Jesus Christ is the same yesterday, today, and forever.

James 4:7
Submit therefore to God. Resist the devil and he will flee from you.

1 Peter 2:24 (NKJV)
Who Himself bore our sins in His own body on the tree, that we, having died to sins, might live for righteousness—by whose stripes you were healed.

1 John 3:8 (NKJV)
He who sins is of the devil, for the devil has sinned from the beginning. For this purpose the Son of God was manifested, that He might destroy the works of the devil.

1 John 4:16–18 (NKJV)
16 And we have known and believed the love that God has for us.
God is love, and he who abides in love abides in God, and God in
him. 17 Love has been perfected among us in this: that we may have
boldness in the day of judgment; because as He is, so are we in this
world. 18 There is no fear in love; but perfect love casts out fear, be-

cause fear involves torment. But he who fears has not been made perfect in love.

1 John 5:14-15 (NKJV)

14 Now this is the confidence that we have in Him, that if we ask
anything according to His will, He hears us. 15 And if we know that
He hears is, whatever we ask, we know that we have the petitions
that we have asked of Him.

3 John 2 (NKJV)

Beloved, I pray that you may prosper in all things and be in health, just as your soul prospers.

Appendix B

Ministry of Jesus

Healing

- *Man with leprosy:* Matthew 8:1–4; Mark 1:40–45; Luke 5:12–15
- *Centurion's servant:* Matthew 8:5–13; Luke 7:1–10
- *Peter's mother-in-law:* Matthew 8:14–15; Mark 1:29–31; Luke 4:38–39
- *Paralyzed man:* Matthew 9:1–8; Mark 2:1–12; Luke 5:17–26
- *Woman with the issue of blood*: Matthew 9:20–22; Mark 5:25–34; Luke 8:43–48
- *Two blind men:* Matthew 9:27–31
- *Man with the shriveled hand:* Matthew 12:9–13; Mark 3:1–5; Luke 6:6–10
- *Canaanite woman's daughter:* Matthew 15:21–28; Mark 7:24–30
- *Blind Bartimaeus:* Matthew 20:29–34; Mark 10:46–52; Luke 18:35–43
- *Deaf/mute man:* Mark 7:31–37
- *Blind man at Bethsaida:* Mark 8:22–26
- *Crippled woman:* Luke 13:10–17
- *Man with dropsy:* Luke 14:1–14
- *Ten lepers:* Luke 17:11–19
- *High priest's servant:* Luke 22:49–51
- *Official's son:* John 4:46–54
- *Sick man at pool of Bethesda:* John 5:1–15
- *Man born blind:* John 9:1–41

Healing/Deliverance

- *Possessed man in the Gadarenes:* Matthew 8:28–34; Mark 5:1–20; Luke 8:26–39
- *Mute demon-possessed man:* Matthew 9:32–33
- *Blind and mute possessed man:* Matthew 12:22–23
- *Possessed boy with seizures:* Matthew 17:14–21; Mark 9:14–29; Luke 9:37–42

Raising the Dead

- *Jairus' daughter:* Matthew 9:18–19, 23–26; Mark 5:21–24, 35–43; Luke 8:40–42, 49–56
- *Widow's son:* Luke 7:11–17
- *Lazarus:* John 11:1–44

Appendix C

Recommended Books

Healing

- Bosworth, F. F. *Christ the Healer*. Grand Rapids, MI: Chosen Books, 1924, 1948.
- Capps, Charles. *God's Creative Power for Healing*. Shippensburg, PA: Harrison House Publishers, 2020.
- Freudiger, Amy Keesee. *The 30-Day Healing Dare Daily Devotional*. United States: Honest Beauty Publishing, 2021.
- Osborn, T. L. *Healing the Sick*. Shippensburg, PA: Harrison House Publishers, 2022.
- Wigglesworth, Smith. *Smith Wigglesworth on Healing*. New Kensington, PA: Whitaker House, 1999.

Faith Building

- Bartleman, Frank. *Azusa Street: An Eyewitness Account to the Birth of the Pentecostal Revival*. New Kensington, PA: Whitaker House, 2000.
- Heflin, Edith Ward. *I Serve the God of Miracles: 80 Years of the Miraculous*. Shippensburg, PA: Destiny Image Publishers, 1991.
- Liardon, Roberts, ed. *God's Generals: The Healing Evangelists*. New Kensington, PA: Whitaker House, 2011.
- Liardon, Roberts, ed. *God's Generals: Why They Succeeded and Why Some Failed*. Tulsa, OK: Albury Publishing, 1996.

- Liardon, Roberts, ed. *John G. Lake: The Complete Collection of His Life Teachings*. Tulsa, OK: Albury Publishing, 1999.
- Liardon, Roberts, ed. *Maria Woodworth-Etter: The Complete Collection of Her Life Teachings*. Shippensburg, PA: Harrison House Publishers, 2021.
- Liardon, Roberts, ed. *Smith Wigglesworth: The Complete Collection of His Life Teachings*. New Kensington, PA: Whitaker House, 2008.
- Sumrall, Lester. *Ask and Ye Shall Receive*. New Kensington, PA: Whitaker House, 1996.
- Wigglesworth, Smith. *Ever Increasing Faith*. Eastford, CT: Martino Publishing, 2011.
- Woodworth-Etter, Maria. *Signs and Wonders*. New Kensington, PA: Whitaker House, 1997.

Identity in Christ

- Bevere, Lisa. *Fiercely Loved: God's Wild Thoughts about You*. Grand Rapids, MI: Revell, a division of Baker Publishing Group, 2022.
- Bevere, Lisa. *Without Rival: Incomparably Made, Uniquely Loved, Powerfully Purposed*. Grand Rapids, MI: Revell, a division of Baker Publishing Group, 2016.
- Hagin, Kenneth E. *The Believer's Authority*. Garland, TX: Kenneth Hagin Ministries, 1985.
- Mathis, Jill. *My Identity in Christ: A Journaling Devotional*. United States: Independently published, 2022.
- Wommack, Andrew. *The Believer's Authority: What You Didn't Learn in Church*. Tulsa, OK: Harrison House Publishers, 2009.

Various Topics

- Bevere, John. *The Bait of Satan: Living Free from the Deadly Trap of Offense*. Lake Mary, FL: Charisma House, 2014.

- Bevere, John. *Extraordinary: The Life You're Meant to Live*. Colorado Springs, CO: WaterBrook Press, 2009.
- Bevere, John. *Relentless: The Power You Need to Never Give Up*. Colorado Springs, CO: WaterBrook Press, 2011.
- Bevere, John. *Under Cover: Why Your Response to Leadership Determines Your Future*. Nashville, TN: Emanate Books, 2001, 2018.
- Hagin, Kenneth E. *Zoe: The God-Kind of Life*. Garland, TX: Faith Library Publications, 1981.
- Johnson, Bill. *The Supernatural Power of a Transformed Mind: Access to a Life of Miracles*. Shippensburg, PA: Destiny Image Publishers, 2014.
- Joyner, Rick. *The Final Quest Trilogy*. Alma, MI: Morning Star Publications, 2016.
- Kirkwood, Kerry. *The Power of Blessing*. Shippensburg, PA: Destiny Image Publishers, 2010.
- Russell, Corrie. *Teach Us to Pray: Prayer That Accesses Heaven and Changes Earth*. Shippensburg, PA: Destiny Image Publishers, 2020.
- Smith, Malcolm. *The Power of the Blood Covenant: Uncover the Secret Strength in God's Eternal Oath*. Tulsa, OK: Harrison House Publishers, 2002.
- Smith, Todd. *Come Alive Dry Bones: The Pathway to the Next Great Awakening*. United States: Independently published, 2021.
- Smith, Todd. *Creating a Habitation for God's Glory*. Shippensburg, PA: Destiny Image Publishers, 2020.
- Smith, Todd. *Unless We Pray*. Shippensburg, PA: Destiny Image Publishers, 2022.
- Snodgrass, Derrick. *The Supernatural Power of Tears: Turning Our Hearts back to the Father*. United States: Independently published, 2020.

- Sumrall, Lester. *The Gifts and Ministries of the Holy Spirit*. New Kensington, PA: Whitaker House, 2005.
- Wommack, Andrew. *Living in the Balance of Grace & Faith*. Tulsa, OK: Harrison House Publishers, 2009.
- Woodworth-Etter, Maria. *The Holy Spirit: Experiencing the Power of the Spirit in Signs, Wonders, and Miracles*. New Kensington, PA: Whitaker House, 1998.

Bible Study Materials

- The Bible (I recommend a translation you can understand)
- A paraphrase Bible: The Passion Translation or The Message (not recommended alone without another translation)
- *Rose Book of Bible Charts, Maps, & Time Lines*. Torrance, CA: Rose Publishing, 2015.
- Strong, James. *The New Strong's Expanded, Exhaustive Concordance of the Bible*. Nashville, TN: Thomas Nelson, 2001.
- Warren, Rick. *Rick Warren's Bible Study Methods: Twelve Ways You Can Unlock God's Word*. Grand Rapids, MI: Zondervan, 1981, 2006.

Learn more at **Kineo Ministry Training Center,** kineomtc.com

This is not an exhaustive list. I am sure I left off many great books, but these are some of the books that remain on my desk shelf, that have transformed my thinking, and that made me reach for more of God.

If an author was mentioned above, I most likely have many of their books, and I recommend you search their websites for other books they have written that may interest you and help you grow in other areas.

Bibliography

Bosworth, F. F. *Christ the Healer.* Grand Rapids, MI: Baker Book House Company, 1973.

Carter, Howard. *Questions & Answers on Spiritual Gifts.* Tulsa, OK: Harrison House, 1976.

Liardon, Roberts, ed. *The Collected Works of John G. Lake.* Tulsa, OK: Albury Publishing, 1999.

Liardon, Roberts, ed. *God's Generals: Why They Succeeded and Why Some Failed.* Tulsa, OK: Albury Publishing, 1996.

Liardon, Roberts, ed. *God's Generals: The Healing Evangelists.* New Kensington, PA: Whitaker House, 2011.

Merriam-Webster.com Dictionary. https://www.merriam-webster.com/

Strong, James. *The New Strong's Expanded Exhaustive Concordance of the Bible: Red Letter Edition.* Nashville, TN: Thomas Nelson Publishers, 2010.

Webster, Noah. *Webster's 1828 Dictionary.* San Francisco, CA: Foundation for American Christian Education, retrieved from https://webstersdictionary1828.com.

Notes

About the Author

Georgianne Summer served as a nurse for over twenty years. She obtained her Bachelor of Science in Nursing at Emory University and her Doctor of Nursing Practice at Augusta University. Georgianne holds diplomas in biblical theology, advanced biblical studies, and theological historical studies from Kineo Ministry Training Center. As a nursing professional, she has been published in *The Nurse Practitioner Journal* and the *Virginia Henderson Global Nursing e-Repository*. Georgianne currently resides in her home state of Georgia and enjoys being a daughter, a wife, a mother, and a grandmother. She is the founder of He Healed All Ministries, with the mission to fulfill the mandate of Matthew 10:8: "Heal the sick, raise the dead, cleanse the lepers, cast out demons. Freely you have received, freely give."

mailing address:	He Healed All Ministries Inc. 113 S. Perry Street, Suite 206 #9266 Lawrenceville, Georgia 30046
website:	Hehealedall.org
email:	gsummer@hehealedall.org

Notes

Notes

Notes